Har  ıt:

Heaven & Hell

By: Only A. Guy

Hard Questions About: Heaven & Hell

Published by VIP Ink Publishing

Cover Art and Editing By Whyte Lady Designs L.L.C.

www.onlyaguy.com
www.facebook.com/onlyaguy
www.twitter.com/onlyaguy1

www.vipinkpublishing.com

ISBN 13: 978-0-9847382-4-3
ISBN:0-9847382-4-3

Printed in the USA.

If you like this book here are some others coming out by this author you may find enjoyable as well as educational:

2011
HARD QUESTIONS ABOUT GOD
HARD QUESTIONS ABOUT JESUS
THE BOOK OF PRAYERS

2012
HARD QUESTIONS ABOUT THE HOLY SPIRIT
HARD QUESTIONS ABOUT HEAVEN AND HELL
HARD QUESTIONS ABOUT ANGELS AND DEMONS
HARD QUESTIONS ABOUT SALVATION
HOPE IN A LOST AND FALLEN WORLD

2013
HARD QUESTIONS ABOUT THE END TIMES
HARD QUESTIONS ABOUT CHRISTIANITY
HARD QUESTIONS ABOUT CREATION
HARD QUESTIONS ABOUT HUMANITY

2014
HARD QUESTIONS ABOUT LIFE'S DECISIONS
HARD QUESTIONS ABOUT CULTS AND RELIGIONS
HARD QUESTIONS ABOUT FALSE DOCTRINE
HARD QUESTIONS ABOUT PRAYER
HARD QUESTIONS ABOUT SIN

1. Question: "Is there life after death?"

The existence of life after death is a universal question. Job speaks for all of us by stating, *"Man born of woman is of few days and full of trouble. He springs up like a flower and withers away; like a fleeting shadow, he does not endure....If a man dies, will he live again?" (Job 14:1-2, 14)*. Like Job, all of us have been challenged by this question. Exactly what happens to us after we die? Do we simply cease to exist? Is life a revolving door of departing and returning to earth in order to eventually achieve personal greatness? Does everyone go to the same place, or do we go to different places? Is there really a heaven and hell?

The Bible tells us that there is not only life after death, but eternal life so glorious that *"no eye has seen, no ear has heard, and no mind has imagined what God has prepared for those who love him" (1 Corinthians 2:9)*. Jesus Christ, God in the flesh, came to the earth to give us this gift of eternal life. *"But he was pierced for our transgressions, he was crushed for our iniquities; the punishment that brought us peace was upon him, and by his wounds we are healed" (Isaiah 53:5)*. Jesus took on the punishment that all of us deserve and sacrificed His life to pay the penalty for our sin. Three days later, He proved Himself victorious over death by rising from the grave. He remained on the earth for forty days and was witnessed by thousands before ascending to heaven. *Romans 4:25* says, *"He was delivered over to death for our sins and was raised to life for our justification."*

The resurrection of the Christ is a well-documented event. The apostle Paul challenged people to question eyewitnesses for its validity, and no one was able to contest its truth. The resurrection is the cornerstone of the Christian faith. Because Christ was raised from the dead, we can have faith that we too will be resurrected. The resurrection of Jesus Christ is the ultimate proof of life after death. Christ was only the first of a great harvest of those who will be raised to life again. Physical death came through one man, Adam, to whom we are all related. But all who have been adopted into God's family through faith in Jesus Christ will be given new life *(1 Corinthians 15:20-22)*. Just as God raised up Jesus' body, so will our bodies be resurrected upon Jesus' return *(1 Corinthians 6:14)*.

Although we will all be eventually resurrected, not everyone will go to heaven. A choice must be made by each person in this life, and this

1

choice will determine one's eternal destination. The Bible says that it is appointed for us to die only once, and after that will come judgment *(Hebrews 9:27)*. Those who have been made righteous by faith in Christ will go into eternal life in heaven, but those who reject Christ as Savior will be sent to eternal punishment in hell *(Matthew 25:46)*. Hell, like heaven, is not simply a state of existence, but a literal place. It is a place where the unrighteous will experience never-ending, eternal wrath from God. Hell is described as a bottomless pit *(Luke 8:31; Revelation 9:1)* and a lake of fire, burning with sulfur, where the inhabitants will be tormented day and night forever and ever *(Revelation 20:10)*. In hell, there will be weeping and gnashing of teeth, indicating intense grief and anger *(Matthew 13:42)*.

God takes no pleasure in the death of the wicked, but desires them to turn from their wicked ways so that they can live *(Ezekiel 33:11)*. But He will not force us into submission; if we choose to reject Him, He accepts our decision to live eternally apart from Him. Life on earth is a test, a preparation for what is to come. For believers, life after death is eternal life in heaven with God. For unbelievers, life after death is eternity in the lake of fire. How can we receive eternal life after death and avoid an eternity in the lake of fire? There is only one way—through faith and trust in Jesus Christ. Jesus said, *"I am the resurrection and the life. He who believes in me will live, even though he dies; and whoever lives and believes in me will never die..." (John 11:25-26)*.

The free gift of eternal life is available to all. *"Whoever believes in the Son has eternal life, but whoever rejects the Son will not see life, for God's wrath remains on him" (John 3:36)*. We will not be given the opportunity to accept God's gift of salvation after death. Our eternal destination is determined in our earthly lifetimes by our reception or rejection of Jesus Christ. *"I tell you, now is the time of God's favor, now is the day of salvation" (2 Corinthians 6:2)*. If we trust the death of Jesus Christ as the full payment for our sin against God, we are guaranteed not only a meaningful life on earth, but also eternal life after death, in the glorious presence of Christ.

2. Question: "Is there an afterlife?"

The book of Job asks the question about an afterlife very simply: *"If a man dies, will he live again?" (Job 14:14)*. Asking the question is easy, but the difficult part is finding someone to answer the question with authority and experience. "Death and taxes" have been said to be the two universals that everyone living can expect to deal with. But while everyone is handled somewhat differently by government taxation, death is the great equalizer that treats everyone the same.

Because of this, it's not uncommon for people to be afraid of death. The ancient philosopher Epicurus (341–270 BC) recognized that the fear of death was present in everybody and therefore he sought a way to remove that fear. Epicurus taught that humanity not need fear death because human beings are nothing more than a composition of atoms, which at death simply disperse, and that is the end of things. Epicurus didn't believe there were any gods to fear or anything to face once a person breathed their last. His teaching of maximum pleasure in this life with minimum pain and suffering dictated that everything ends when death occurred.

One of the groups the Apostle Paul encountered in his trip to Athens were the Epicureans, who listened to Paul's Mars Hill address up until he mentioned the resurrection of Jesus and then abruptly ended the discussion *(Acts 17:32)*. They had been bathed in their teacher's philosophy and likely knew well the statement made by Apollos the Epicurean who said during the founding of the Areopagus where Paul was speaking, *"When the dust has soaked up a person's blood, once he is dead, there is no resurrection."*

But after thousands of years since that time, the fear of death remains fixed in many people. The book of Job describes death as the *"king of terrors" (Job 18:14)*. This fact is visible in the movie "The Bucket List" where the character played by Jack Nicholson, trying to come to grips with dying, says: "We all want to go on forever, don't we? We fear the unknown. Everybody goes to that wall, yet nobody knows what's on the other side. That's why we fear death."

But one person has gone to that wall, gone through to the other side, and come back to tell us what to expect. He alone possesses the authority and knowledge to tell everyone the truth about the afterlife.

A. The Expert on the Afterlife

From a historical perspective, no historical scholar disputes the life of Jesus of Nazareth. There is no debate about His teachings or the fact that He reportedly did miraculous things, and there is universal agreement that He was put to death by crucifixion under the Roman prefect Pontius Pilate. Jesus went to the wall of death and through to the other side. The resurrection puts Jesus in a place of being the sole authority and witness able to answer the question, "Is there an afterlife?" And what does He have to say? Christ makes three basic statements about the subject of life after death:

1) There is an afterlife.
2) When a person dies, there are two different eternities to which he/she will go.
3) There is a way to ensure a positive experience after death.

First, Christ most certainly affirms there is an afterlife in a number of biblical passages. For example, in an encounter with the Sadducees who denied the teaching of resurrection, Christ rebuked them by saying, *"Regarding the fact that the dead rise again, have you not read in the book of Moses, in the passage about the burning bush, how God spoke to him, saying, 'I am the God of Abraham, and the God of Isaac, and the God of Jacob'? He is not the God of the dead, but of the living; you are greatly mistaken" (Mark 12:26-27).* Jesus clearly told them that those who have died centuries before are very much alive with God at that moment.

In another passage, Jesus comforts His disciples (and us) by telling them specifically that they can look forward to being with Him in Heaven: *"Do not let your heart be troubled; believe in God, believe also in Me. In My Father's house are many dwelling places; if it were not so, I would have told you; for I go to prepare a place for you. If I go and prepare a place for you, I will come again and receive you to Myself, that where I am, there you may be also. And you know the way where I am going" (John 14:1-4).*

B. Two Eternal Destinies

Jesus also speaks authoritatively about what types of destinies

4

await every person that dies: one with God and one without God. In Luke's account of the rich man and Lazarus, Jesus says, *"Now the poor man died and was carried away by the angels to Abraham's bosom; and the rich man also died and was buried. In Hades he lifted up his eyes, being in torment, and saw Abraham far away and Lazarus in his bosom"* (Luke 16:22–23). One aspect of the story worth noting is that there is no intermediate state for those who die; they go directly to their eternal destiny. As the writer of Hebrews says, *"It is appointed for men to die once and after this comes judgment"* (Hebrews 9:27).

Jesus speaks about the two final destinies again when He is confronted by the religious leaders in John: *"Truly, truly, I say to you, an hour is coming and now is, when the dead will hear the voice of the Son of God, and those who hear will live. For just as the Father has life in Himself, even so He gave to the Son also to have life in Himself; and He gave Him authority to execute judgment, because He is the Son of Man. Do not marvel at this; for an hour is coming, in which all who are in the tombs will hear His voice, and will come forth; those who did the good deeds to a resurrection of life, those who committed the evil deeds to a resurrection of judgment"* (John 5:25-29). Christ restates the matter very plainly in Matthew when He says, *"These [unbelievers] will go away into eternal punishment, but the righteous into eternal life"* (Matthew 25:46).

C. What Determines Our Eternal Destination?

Jesus also is clear on what determines each person's eternal destination—whether they have faith in God and what they do with respect to Christ. The book of John contains many statements made by Jesus on this subject, with perhaps the most famous being these: *"As Moses lifted up the serpent in the wilderness, even so must the Son of Man be lifted up; so that whoever believes will in Him have eternal life. For God so loved the world, that He gave His only begotten Son, that whoever believes in Him shall not perish, but have eternal life. For God did not send the Son into the world to judge the world, but that the world might be saved through Him. He who believes in Him is not judged; he who does not believe has been judged already, because he has not believed in the name of the only begotten Son of God" (John 3:14-18).*

For those who repent and receive Christ as their Savior and Lord, the afterlife will consist of an eternity spent with God. But for those who reject Christ, their destiny will be spent away from God's presence. Jesus contrasts these two destinies in the end of the Sermon on the Mount: *"Enter through the narrow gate; for the gate is wide and the way is broad that leads to destruction, and there are many who enter through it. For the gate is small and the way is narrow that leads to life, and there are few who find it" (Matthew 7:13-14).*

D. The Afterlife – Conclusions

Speaking about life after death, G. B. Hardy, a Canadian Scientist, once said, "I have only two questions to ask. One, has anyone ever defeated death? Two, did he make a way for me to do it also?" The answer to both of Hardy's questions is "yes." One Person has both defeated death and provided a way for everyone who puts their trust in Him to overcome it as well. Epicurus may have believed that everyone fears death, but the truth is no one who trusts in Christ needs to be afraid. Rejoicing in this fact, the Apostle Paul wrote, *"When the perishable has been clothed with the imperishable, and the mortal with immortality, then the saying that is written will come true: "Death has been swallowed up in victory.' 'Where, O death, is your victory? Where, O death, is your sting?'" (1 Corinthians 15:54–55).*

3. Question: "How can I not go to hell?"

Not going to hell is easier than you think. Some people believe they have to obey the Ten Commandments for their entire lives to not go to hell. Some people believe they must observe certain rites and rituals in order to not go to hell. Some people believe there is no way we can know for sure whether or not we will go to hell. None of these views are correct. The Bible is very clear on how a person can avoid going to hell after death.

The Bible describes hell as a terrifying and horrible place. Hell is described as *"eternal fire" (Matthew 25:41)*, *"unquenchable fire" (Matthew 3:12)*, *"shame and everlasting contempt" (Daniel 12:2)*, a place where *"the fire is not quenched" (Mark 9:44-49)*, and *"everlasting destruction" (2 Thessalonians 1:9)*. *Revelation 20:10* describes hell as a *"lake of burning sulfur"* where the wicked are *"tormented day and night forever and ever."* Obviously, hell is a place we should avoid.

Why does hell even exist, and why does God send some people there? The Bible tells us that God "prepared" hell for the devil and the fallen angels after they rebelled against Him *(Matthew 25:41)*. Those who refuse God's offer of forgiveness will suffer the same eternal destiny of the devil and the fallen angels. Why is hell necessary? All sin is ultimately against God *(Psalm 51:4)*, and since God is an infinite and eternal being, only an infinite and eternal penalty is sufficient. Hell is the place where God's holy and righteous demands of justice are carried out. Hell is where God condemns sin and all those who reject Him. The Bible makes it clear that we have all sinned *(Ecclesiastes 7:20; Romans 3:10-23)*, so, as a result, we all deserve to go to hell.

So, how can we not go to hell? Since only an infinite and eternal penalty is sufficient, an infinite and eternal price must be paid. God became a human being in the Person of Jesus Christ *(John 1:1, 14)*. In Jesus Christ, God lived among us, taught us, and healed us—but those things were not His ultimate mission. God became a human being so that He could die for us. Jesus, God in human form, died on the cross. As God, His death was infinite and eternal in value, paying the full price for sin *(1 John 2:2)*. God invites us to receive Jesus Christ as Savior, accepting His death as the full and just payment for our sins. God promises that anyone who believes in Jesus *(John 3:16)*, trusting Him alone as the Savior *(John 14:6)*, will be saved, i.e., not go to hell.

God does not want anyone to go to hell *(2 Peter 3:9)*. That is why God made the ultimate, perfect, and sufficient sacrifice on our behalf. If you want to not go to hell, receive Jesus as your Savior. It is as simple as that. Tell God that you recognize that you are a sinner and that you deserve to go to hell. Declare to God that you are trusting in Jesus Christ as your Savior. Thank God for providing for your salvation and deliverance from hell. Simple faith, trusting in Jesus Christ as the Savior, is how you can avoid going to hell!

4. Question: "Will we be able to see and know our friends and family members in Heaven?"

Many people say that the first thing they want to do when they arrive in heaven is see all their friends and loved ones who have passed on before them. In eternity, there will be plenty of time to see, know, and spend time with our friends and family members. However, that will not be our primary focus in heaven. We will be far more occupied with worshipping God and enjoying the wonders of heaven. Our reunions with loved ones are more likely to be filled with recounting the grace and glory of God in our lives, His wondrous love, and His mighty works. We will rejoice all the more because we can praise and worship the Lord in the company of other believers, especially those we loved on earth.

What does the Bible say about whether we will be able to recognize people in the afterlife? King Saul recognized Samuel when the witch of Endor summoned Samuel from the realm of the dead *(1 Samuel 28:8-17)*. When David's infant son died, David declared, *"I will go to him, but he will not return to me" (2 Samuel 12:23)*. David assumed that he would be able to recognize his son in heaven, despite the fact that he died as a baby. In *Luke 16:19-31*, Abraham, Lazarus, and the rich man were all recognizable after death. At the transfiguration Moses and Elijah were recognizable *(Matthew 17:3-4)*. In these examples, the Bible does seem to indicate that we will be recognizable after death.

The Bible declares that when we arrive in heaven, we will *"be like him [Jesus]; for we shall see him as he is" (1 John 3:2)*. Just as our earthly bodies were of the first man Adam, so will our resurrection bodies be just like Christ's *(1 Corinthians 15:47)*. *"And just as we have borne the likeness of the earthly man, so shall we bear the likeness of the man from heaven. For the perishable must clothe itself with the imperishable, and the mortal with immortality" (1 Corinthians 15:49, 53)*. Many people recognized Jesus after His resurrection *(John 20:16, 20; 21:12; 1 Corinthians 15:4-7)*. If Jesus was recognizable in His glorified body, we also will be recognizable in our glorified bodies. Being able to see our loved ones is a glorious aspect of heaven, but heaven is far more about God, and far less about us. What a pleasure it will be to be reunited with our loved ones and worship God with them for all eternity.

5. Question: "What happens after death?"

Within the Christian faith, there is a significant amount of confusion regarding what happens after death. Some hold that after death, everyone "sleeps" until the final judgment, after which everyone will be sent to heaven or hell. Others believe that at the moment of death, people are instantly judged and sent to their eternal destinations. Still others claim that when people die, their souls/spirits are sent to a "temporary" heaven or hell, to await the final resurrection, the final judgment, and then the finality of their eternal destination. So, what exactly does the Bible say happens after death?

First, for the believer in Jesus Christ, the Bible tells us that after death believers' souls/spirits are taken to heaven, because their sins are forgiven by having received Christ as Savior *(John 3:16, 18, 36)*. For believers, death is to be *"away from the body and at home with the Lord" (2 Corinthians 5:6-8; Philippians 1:23)*. However, passages such as *1 Corinthians 15:50-54* and *1 Thessalonians 4:13-17* describe believers being resurrected and given glorified bodies. If believers go to be with Christ immediately after death, what is the purpose of this resurrection? It seems that while the souls/spirits of believers go to be with Christ immediately after death, the physical body remains in the grave "sleeping." At the resurrection of believers, the physical body is resurrected, glorified, and then reunited with the soul/spirit. This reunited and glorified body-soul-spirit will be the possession of believers for eternity in the new heavens and new earth *(Revelation 21-22)*.

Second, for those who do not receive Jesus Christ as Savior, death means everlasting punishment. However, similar to the destiny of believers, unbelievers also seem to be sent immediately to a temporary holding place, to await their final resurrection, judgment, and eternal destiny. *Luke 16:22-23* describes a rich man being tormented immediately after death. *Revelation 20:11-15* describes all the unbelieving dead being resurrected, judged at the great white throne, and then being cast into the lake of fire. Unbelievers, then, are not sent to hell (the lake of fire) immediately after death, but rather are in a temporary realm of judgment and condemnation. However, even though unbelievers are not instantly sent to the lake of fire, their immediate fate after death is not a pleasant one. The rich man cried out, *"I am in agony in this fire" (Luke 16:24)*.

Therefore, after death, a person resides in a "temporary" heaven or hell. After this temporary realm, at the final resurrection, a person's eternal destiny will not change. The precise "location" of that eternal destiny is what changes. Believers will ultimately be granted entrance into the new heavens and new earth *(Revelation 21:1)*. Unbelievers will ultimately be sent to the lake of fire *(Revelation 20:11-15)*. These are the final, eternal destinations of all people—based entirely on whether or not they had trusted Jesus Christ alone for salvation *(Matthew 25:46; John 3:36)*.

6. Question: "How can I know for sure that I will go to Heaven when I die?"

Do you know for certain that you have eternal life and that you will go to Heaven when you die? God wants you to be sure! The Bible says: *"I write these things to you who believe in the name of the Son of God so that you may know that you have eternal life" (1 John 5:13)*. Suppose you were standing before God right now and He asked you, "Why should I let you into Heaven?" What would you say? You may not know what to reply. What you need to know is that God loves us and has provided a way that we can know for sure where we will spend eternity. The Bible states it this way: *"For God so loved the world that He gave His only Son, that whoever believes in Him shall not perish but have eternal life" (John 3:16)*.

We have to first understand the problem that is keeping us from Heaven. The problem is this - our sinful nature keeps us from having a relationship with God. We are sinners by nature and by choice. *"For all have sinned and fall short of the glory of God" (Romans 3:23)*. We cannot save ourselves. *"For by grace are you saved, through faith, and this not of yourselves – it is the gift of God. Not by works, so that no one can boast" (Ephesians 2:8-9)*. We deserve death and hell. *"For the wages of sin is death" (Romans 6:23)*.

God is holy and just and must punish sin, yet He loves us and has provided forgiveness for our sin. Jesus said: *"I am the way and the truth and the life. No one comes to the Father except through me" (John*

10

14:6). Jesus died for us on the cross: *"For Christ died for sins once for all, the righteous for the unrighteous to bring you to God" (1 Peter 3:18)*. Jesus was resurrected from the dead: *"He was delivered over to death for our sins and was raised to life for our justification" (Romans 4:25)*.

So, back to the original question – "How can I know for sure that I will go to Heaven when I die?" The answer is this – believe in the Lord Jesus Christ and you will be saved *(Acts 16:31)*. *"To all who received Him, to those who believed in His Name, He gave the right to become children of God" (John 1:12)*. You can receive eternal life as a FREE gift. *"The gift of God is eternal life in Christ Jesus our Lord" (Romans 6:23)*. You can live a full and meaningful life right now. Jesus said: *"I have come that they may have life, and have it to the full" (John 10:10)*. You can spend eternity with Jesus in Heaven, for He promised: *"And if I go and prepare a place for you, I will come back and take you to be with me that you may also be where I am" (John 14:3)*.

If you want to accept Jesus Christ as your Savior and receive forgiveness from God, here is prayer you can pray. Saying this prayer or any other prayer will not save you. It is only trusting in Jesus Christ that can provide forgiveness of sins. This prayer is simply a way to express to God your faith in Him and thank Him for providing for your forgiveness. "God, I know that I have sinned against You and am deserving of punishment. But Jesus Christ took the punishment that I deserve so that through faith in Him I could be forgiven. I place my trust in You for salvation. Thank You for Your wonderful grace and forgiveness! Amen!"

7. Question: "How can I overcome the fear of death? How can I stop being scared of dying?"

Even the most secure, devout believer can have occasions when they fear death. It is hard-wired into our systems to avoid death. And death was not an original part of God's plan for His creation. We were made to be whole and holy, living in paradise in communion with Him. The introduction of death was a necessary response to the admittance of sin into the world. It is a grace that we die. If we didn't, we would have to live in a sinful world for all eternity.

Knowing that in your head doesn't necessarily counteract the visceral reaction to the thought of your own mortality. The fragility of our physical bodies and the sudden cessation of life are violent reminders of our lack of control in a large, dangerous world. We do have a great hope, that He Who is in us is greater than he who is in the world *(1 John 4:4)*. And He did go to prepare a place for us so that we can join Him *(John 14:2)*. But it might help to consider the more immediate, practical considerations we're faced with.

Beginning with, what is the actual fear? There are several aspects of death that can potentially cause fear. Fortunately, God has an answer for each of them.

1) **Fear of the unknown**
   What exactly does it feel like to die? What can you see as your life leaves your physical body? How will it come about? Is it anything like people have reported—a bright light? A group of relatives? No one knows for certain what it feels like, but the Bible does describe what happens. 2 Corinthians 5:6-8 and Philippians 1:23 say that when we leave our body, we are at home with the Lord. What a reassuring thought! We will stay in this state until Christ comes and resurrects the believers (1 Corinthians 15:20-22, 6:14) when we will be given a new, glorified body.

2) **Fear of loss of control**
   By the time humans reach adulthood, they have a pretty good idea how to interact with the world around them. They know how to find what they need, get to where they want to be, and interact with others in a way that fulfills their intent. Many though, even those who profess a trust in God, are so fearful of not getting what they need that they feel they have no choice but to manipulate their surroundings and the people around them to their benefit. We have all met men and women who abuse and grasp out of fear. They don't trust God to provide for their needs, so they take care of things themselves. They don't trust others to give them consideration, so they demand what they think they need. How much more they must fear the loss of control upon their deaths. As Jesus said to Peter, describing how he would die, "Truly, truly, I say to

you, when you were younger, you used to gird yourself and walk wherever you wished; but when you grow old, you will stretch out your hands and someone else will gird you, and bring you where you do not wish to go" (John 21:18). Before Peter got this warning, he denied Jesus out of fear. Directly after, he reacted by demanding to know how John was going to die. But after Jesus returned to heaven, Peter took the gift of the Holy Spirit and became a new person—one whose passion for Christ's message far outstripped his need to control his surroundings (Acts 5:17-42). The Holy Spirit alone gave him the strength to face whatever challenges he might face.

3) **Fear for those left behind**
The Christian view of death is "separation." Ultimate death is separation from God. With physical death, we will be separated from our loved ones on Earth for a time. If they are also Christians, we know that the separation will be a short blink of an eye compared to the eternity we'll spend with them in heaven. If they are not Christians, that will not be the case. Our commission, then, becomes to use this time together to talk to them about where they will go when they die. Ultimately, however, the decision rests with them. Just as God gives them the room to choose, we must also.

4) **Fear of the act of dying**
Few of us know how we will die. Quick and painless, in our sleep, a long drawn out illness—the mystery of it, the inability to prepare, can be frightening. If we do know, if we've been diagnosed with a terminal illness, it can still be scary. But it is only a moment. A moment nearly everyone has gone through or will go through. And, when that moment is over, we can claim Philippians 3:20-21: "But our citizenship is in heaven. And we eagerly await a Savior from there, the Lord Jesus Christ, who, by the power that enables him to bring everything under his control, will transform our lowly bodies so that they will be like his glorious body." Often, being informed and actively participating can help assuage fear. You can take steps to prepare yourself and those around you.

OVERCOMING THE FEAR OF DEATH

a) **Practical steps** - Many people believe they shouldn't die because they have too much to live for. Often, this means they have responsibilities and unfinished business that wouldn't be taken care of if they were gone. But having people and things you are responsible for won't keep you from dying if it's your time. Doing what you can to make sure they're seen to can alleviate fear. If you have a business or children or other dependents, consider their care. Decide who will take over your role and work with that person to come up with a plan. Look into a will or a trust. Make sure all of your necessary paperwork is organized and easy to find. Reconcile broken relationships before you're unable to. But don't live for dying. There's a difference between taking reasonable steps and obsessing.

b) **Physical steps** - If you have strong feelings about what you want to happen to you should you become incapacitated, express them now. It's entirely possible that during the course of an illness or injury, you'll lose control over the situation and be unable to make your wishes known. Get a living will. Let those closest to you know what you want—or at least tell them where it's written down. Choose someone you trust to be authorized to make decisions for you should you become unable.

c) **Spiritual steps** - These are all steps to keep up responsibilities or maintain a measure of control in the worldly realm, but they don't get to the meat of the matter. The most important thing to remember regarding death is the truth about life. You love your family and care for them, but God loves them more. You may worry about your Earthly legacy, but God's more concerned with a kingdom perspective. All the paperwork in the world won't bring the peace of mind of once simple action; **abide**. In the middle of living this life, with these people, in this world, it's difficult to keep in mind that this is just a temporary condition, and not a very good one at that. *1 John 2:15-17* says, *"Do not love the world nor the things in the world. If anyone loves the world, the love of the Father is not in him. For all that is in the world, the lust of the flesh and the lust of the eyes and the boastful pride of life, is not from the Father, but is from the world. The world is passing away, and also its lusts; but the one who does the will of God lives forever."* How we remember this is by abiding *(1 John 2:24)*. Staying in the truth of His Word, believing what He says about us and the world around us, will give us the proper perspective regarding this life and the one we will receive.

When we are able to keep that kingdom perspective, we'll be able to fulfill *1 John 3:1-3: "See how great a love the Father has bestowed on us, that we would be called children of God; and such we are, for this reason the world does not know us, because it did not know Him. Beloved, now we are children of God, and it has not appeared as yet what we will be. We know that when He appears, we will be like Him, because we will see Him just as He is."* It will be so evident that we do not belong in this world that others will see it, too. We will so take ownership of our position as children of God that we will actively seek the day we can be like Christ and see Him as He is.

8. Question: "What is Heaven like?"

Heaven is a real place described in the Bible. The word "heaven" is found 276 times in the New Testament alone. Scripture refers to three heavens. The apostle Paul was *"caught up to the third heaven,"* but he was prohibited from revealing what he experienced there *(2 Corinthians 12:1-9).*

If a third heaven exists, there must also be two other heavens. The first is most frequently referred to in the Old Testament as the "sky" or the "firmament." This is the heaven that contains clouds, the area that birds fly through. The second heaven is interstellar/outer space, which is the abode of the stars, planets, and other celestial objects *(Genesis 1:14-18).*

The third heaven, the location of which is not revealed, is the dwelling place of God. Jesus promised to prepare a place for true Christians in heaven *(John 14:2).* Heaven is also the destination of Old Testament saints who died trusting God's promise of the Redeemer *(Ephesians 4:8).* Whoever believes in Christ shall never perish but have eternal life *(John 3:16).*

The apostle John was privileged to see and report on the heavenly city *(Revelation 21:10-27).* John witnessed that heaven (the new earth) possesses the *"glory of God" (Revelation 21:11)*, the very presence of God. Because heaven has no night and the Lord Himself is the light, the sun and moon are no longer needed *(Revelation 22:5).*

The city is filled with the brilliance of costly stones and crystal clear jasper. Heaven has twelve gates *(Revelation 21:12)* and twelve foundations *(Revelation 21:14)*. The paradise of the Garden of Eden is restored: the river of the water of life flows freely and the tree of life is available once again, yielding fruit monthly with leaves that "heal the nations" *(Revelation 22:1-2)*. However eloquent John was in his description of heaven, the reality of heaven is beyond the ability of finite man to describe *(1 Corinthians 2:9)*.

Heaven is a place of "no mores." There will be no more tears, no more pain, and no more sorrow *(Revelation 21:4)*. There will be no more separation, because death will be conquered *(Revelation 20:6)*. The best thing about heaven is the presence of our Lord and Savior *(1 John 3:2)*. We will be face to face with the Lamb of God who loved us and sacrificed Himself so that we can enjoy His presence in heaven for eternity.

9. Question: "Is Heaven real?"

Heaven is indeed a real place. The Bible tells us that heaven is God's throne *(Isaiah 66:1; Acts 7:48-49; Matthew 5:34-35)*. After Jesus' resurrection and appearance on earth to His disciples, *"He was taken up into heaven and sat at the right hand of God" (Mark 16:19; Acts 7:55-56)*. *"Christ did not enter a man-made sanctuary that was only a copy of the true one; He entered heaven itself, now to appear for us in God's presence" (Hebrews 9:24)*. Jesus not only went before us, entering on our behalf, but He is alive and has a present ministry in heaven, serving as our high priest in the true tabernacle made by *God (Hebrews 6:19-20; 8:1-2)*.

We are also told by Jesus Himself that there are many rooms in God's house and that He has gone before us to prepare a place for us. We have the assurance of His word that He will one day come back to earth and take us to where He is in heaven *(John 14:1-4)*. Our belief in an eternal home in heaven is based on an explicit promise of Jesus. Heaven is most definitely a real place. Heaven truly does exist.

When people deny the existence of heaven, they deny not only the written Word of God, but they also deny the innermost longings of their own hearts. Paul addressed this issue in his letter to the Corinthians, encouraging them to cling to the hope of heaven so that they would not lose heart. Although we "groan and sigh" in our earthly state, we have the hope of heaven always before us and are eager to get there *(2 Corinthians 5:1-4)*. Paul urged the Corinthians to look forward to their eternal home in heaven, a perspective that would enable them to endure hardships and disappointments in this life. *"For our light and momentary troubles are achieving for us an eternal glory that far outweighs them all. So we fix our eyes not on what is seen, but on what is unseen. For what is seen is temporary, but what is unseen is eternal" (2 Corinthians 4:17-18).*

Just as God has put in men's hearts the knowledge that He exists *(Romans 1:19-20)*, so are we "programmed" to desire heaven. It is the theme of countless books, songs, and works of art. Unfortunately, our sin has barred the way to heaven. Since heaven is the abode of a holy and perfect God, sin has no place there, nor can it be tolerated. Fortunately, God has provided for us the key to open the doors of heaven— Jesus Christ *(John 14:6)*. All who believe in Him and seek forgiveness for sin will find the doors of heaven swung wide open for them. May the future glory of our eternal home motivate us all to serve God faithfully and wholeheartedly. *"Since we have confidence to enter the Most Holy Place by the blood of Jesus by a new and living way opened for us through the curtain, that is his body, and since we have a great high priest over the house of God, let us draw near to God with a sincere heart full of assurance of faith, having our hearts sprinkled to cleanse us from a guilty conscience and having our bodies washed with pure water" (Hebrews 10:19-22).*

10. Question: "Is hell real? Is hell eternal?"

It is interesting that a much higher percentage of people believe in the existence of heaven than believe in the existence of hell. According to the Bible, though, hell is just as real as heaven. The Bible clearly and explicitly teaches that hell is a real place to which the wicked/unbelieving are sent after death. We have all sinned against God *(Romans 3:23)*. The just punishment for that sin is death *(Romans 6:23)*. Since all of our sin is ultimately against God *(Psalm 51:4)*, and since God is an infinite and eternal Being, the punishment for sin, death, must also be infinite and eternal. Hell is this infinite and eternal death which we have earned because of our sin.

The punishment of the wicked dead in hell is described throughout Scripture as *"eternal fire" (Matthew 25:41)*, *"unquenchable fire" (Matthew 3:12)*, *"shame and everlasting contempt" (Daniel 12:2)*, a place where *"the fire is not quenched" (Mark 9:44-49)*, a place of *"torment"* and *"fire" (Luke 16:23-24)*, *"everlasting destruction" (2 Thessalonians 1:9)*, a place where *"the smoke of torment rises forever and ever" (Revelation 14:10-11)*, and a *"lake of burning sulfur"* where the wicked are *"tormented day and night forever and ever" (Revelation 20:10)*.

The punishment of the wicked in hell is as never ending as the bliss of the righteous in heaven. Jesus Himself indicates that punishment in hell is just as everlasting as life in heaven *(Matthew 25:46)*. The wicked are forever subject to the fury and the wrath of God. Those in hell will acknowledge the perfect justice of God *(Psalm 76:10)*. Those who are in hell will know that their punishment is just and that they alone are to blame *(Deuteronomy 32:3-5)*. Yes, hell is real. Yes, hell is a place of torment and punishment that lasts forever and ever, with no end. Praise God that, through Jesus, we can escape this eternal fate *(John 3:16, 18, 36)*.

11. Question: "Are books such as 90 minutes in Heaven and 23 minutes in Hell biblically based?"

Recent best-selling books "Heaven is for Real" by Todd Burpo, "90 Minutes in Heaven" by Don Piper and "23 Minutes in Hell" by Bill Wiese are raising the question "Is God giving people visions of heaven and hell today?" "Is it possible that God is taking people to heaven and/or hell, and then sending them back in order to deliver a message to us?" While the popularity of these new books is bringing the concept to the forefront, the over-arching claim is nothing new. Books such as "A Divine Revelation of Hell" and "A Divine Revelation of Heaven" by Mary Baxter and "We Saw Heaven" by Roberts Liardon have been available for years. The key question is are such claims biblically solid?

First, it is important to note that of course God COULD give a person a vision of heaven or hell. God gave the Apostle Paul just such a vision in *2 Corinthians 12:1-6*. Isaiah had an amazing experience as recorded in *Isaiah 6*. Yes, it is possible that Piper, Wiese, Baxter, and others have truly been to heaven and/or hell and come back. Ultimately, only God knows if these claims are true or the result of misperception, exaggeration, or, worse, outright deception. The only way for us to discern is to compare the visions and experiences with the Word of God.

If God were to truly give a person a vision of heaven or hell, one thing we can know for sure is that it would be in 100% agreement with His Word. A God-given vision of heaven would in no sense contradict Scriptures such as *Revelation 21-22*. Further, if God were to truly give multiple people visions of heaven or hell, the God-given visions would in no sense contradict each other. Yes, the visions could be different and could focus on different details, but they would not contradict one another.

As with any book written by any author, *"test everything. Hold on to the good. Avoid every kind of evil" (1 Thessalonians 5:21-22)*. If you read these books, read with a discerning mind. Always compare what the author says and claims with Scripture. Most importantly, never allow someone else's experience and his interpretation of that experience to shape your understanding of Scripture. Scripture must be used to interpret experience, not the other way around. Be blessed and encouraged by what happened to other people, but do not allow their experiences to be the foundation of your faith or walk with God.

Overall, we found "90 Minutes in Heaven" by Don Piper and "Heaven is for Real" by Todd Burpo to be the most biblical and believable of all the available books. Piper and Burpo seem to approach the issue with humility and honesty. Whether or not the visions were truly from God, the experiences appear to be miraculous. Again, though, read with a healthy amount of discernment and a commitment to the Bible as the absolute source of truth.

When the Apostle Paul was *"caught up to paradise,"* he *"heard inexpressible things, things that man is not permitted to tell" (2 Corinthians 12:4)*. Similarly, the Apostle John *(Revelation 10:3-4)* and the prophet Daniel *(Daniel 8:26; 9:24; 12:4)* were instructed to conceal aspects of the visions they received. It would be quite strange for God to have Paul, Daniel, and John withhold aspects of what He revealed to them, only to, 2000+ years later, give even greater visions, along with permission for full disclosure, to people today. It is our contention that these books claiming visions of and trips to heaven and hell should be viewed skeptically and, most importantly, biblically.

12. Question: "Are there different levels of Heaven?"

The closest thing Scripture says to there being different levels of heaven is found in *2 Corinthians 12:2, "I know a man in Christ who fourteen years ago was caught up to the third heaven. Whether it was in the body or out of the body I do not know—God knows."* Some interpret this as indicating that there are three different levels of heaven, a level for "super-committed Christians" or Christians who have obtained a high level of spirituality, a level for "ordinary" Christians, and a level for Christians who did not serve God faithfully. This view has no basis in Scripture.

Paul is not saying that there are three heavens or even three levels of heaven. In many ancient cultures, people used the term "heaven" to describe three different "realms" - the sky, outer space, and then a spiritual heaven. Although the terms are not specifically biblical, these are commonly known as the terrestrial, telestial, and celestial heavens. Paul was saying that God took him to the "celestial" heavens, as in the realm in which God dwells. The concept of different levels of heaven may have come in part from Dante's Divine Comedy in which the poet describes both heaven and hell as having nine different levels. The Divine Comedy, however, is a fictional work. The idea of different levels of heaven is foreign to Scripture.

Scripture does speak of different rewards in heaven. Jesus said regarding rewards, *"Behold, I am coming soon! My reward is with me, and I will give to everyone according to what he has done" (Revelation 22:12).* Jesus said that when He comes He will have with Him rewards to give to people on the basis of what they have done. This shows us that there will be a time of reward for believers. In *2 Timothy 4:7-8*, we read the words of Paul as he closes out his ministry: *"I have fought the good fight, I have finished the race, I have kept the faith. Now there is in store for me the crown of righteousness, which the Lord, the righteous Judge, will award to me on that day — and not only to me, but also to all who have longed for his appearing."*

Only those works that survive God's refining fire have eternal value and will be worthy of reward. Those valuable works are referred to as *"gold, silver, and costly stones" (1 Corinthians 3:12)* and are those things that are built upon the foundation of faith in Christ. Those works that will not be rewarded are called "wood, hay, and stubble"; these are not evil deeds but shallow activities with no eternal value. Rewards will be distributed at the "judgment seat of Christ," a place where believers' lives will be evaluated for the purpose of rewards. "Judgment" of believers never refers to punishment for sin. Jesus Christ was punished for our sin when He died on the cross, and God said about us: *"I will forgive their wickedness and will remember their sins no more" (Hebrews 8:12).* What a glorious thought! The Christian need never fear punishment, but can look forward to crowns of reward that he can cast at the feet of the Savior. In conclusion, there are not different levels of heaven, but there are different levels of reward in heaven.

13. Question: "Is annihilationism biblical?"

Annihilationism is the belief that unbelievers will not experience an eternity of suffering in hell, but will instead be "extinguished" after death. For many, annihilationism is an attractive belief because of the awfulness of the idea of people spending eternity in hell. While there are some passages that seem to argue for annihilationism, a comprehensive look at what the Bible says about the destiny of the wicked reveals the fact that punishment in hell is eternal. A belief in annihilationism results from a misunderstanding of one or more of the following doctrines:

        1) the consequences of sin,
        2) the justice of God,
        3) the nature of hell.

In relation to the nature of hell, annihilationists misunderstand the meaning of the lake of fire. Obviously, if a human being were cast into a lake of burning lava, he/she would be almost instantly consumed. However, the lake of fire is both a physical and spiritual realm. It is not simply a human body being cast into the lake of fire; it is a human's body, soul, and spirit. A spiritual nature cannot be consumed by physical fire. It seems that the unsaved are resurrected with a body prepared for eternity just as the saved are *(Revelation 20:13; Acts 24:15)*. These bodies are prepared for an eternal fate.

Eternity is another aspect which annihilationists fail to fully comprehend. Annihilationists are correct that the Greek word aionion, which is usually translated "eternal," does not by definition mean "eternal." It specifically refers to an "age" or "eon," a specific period of time. However, it is clear that in New Testament, aionion is sometimes used to refer to an eternal length of time. *Revelation 20:10* speaks of Satan, the beast, and the false prophet being cast into the lake of fire and being tormented *"day and night forever and ever."* It is clear that these three are not *"extinguished"* by being cast into the lake of fire. Why would the fate of the unsaved be any different *(Revelation 20:14-15)*? The most convincing evidence for the eternality of hell is *Matthew 25:46, "Then they [the unsaved] will go away to eternal punishment, but the righteous to eternal life."* In this verse, the same Greek word is used to refer to the destiny of the wicked and the righteous. If the wicked are only tormented for an "age," then the righteous will only experience life in heaven for an "age." If believers will be in heaven forever, unbelievers will be in hell forever.

Another frequent objection to the eternality of hell by annihilationists is that it would be unjust for God to punish unbelievers in hell for eternity for a finite amount of sin. How could it be fair for God to take a person who lived a sinful, 70-year life, and punish him/her for all of eternity? The answer is that our sin bears an eternal consequence because it is committed against an eternal God. When King David committed the sins of adultery and murder he stated, *"Against you, you only, have I sinned and done what is evil in your sight..."* *(Psalm 51:4)*. David had sinned against Bathsheba and Uriah; how could David claim to have only sinned against God? David understood that all sin is ultimately against God. God is an eternal and infinite Being. As a result, all sin against Him is worthy of an eternal punishment. It is not a matter of the length of time we sin, but the character of the God against whom we sin.

A more personal aspect of annihilationism is the idea that we could not possibly be happy in heaven if we knew that some of our loved ones were suffering an eternity of torment in hell. However, when we arrive in heaven, we will not have anything to complain about or be saddened by. *Revelation 21:4* tells us, *"He will wipe every tear from their eyes. There will be no more death or mourning or crying or pain, for the old order of things has passed away."* If some of our loved ones are not in heaven, we will be in 100 percent complete agreement that they do not belong there and that they are condemned by their own refusal to accept Jesus Christ as their Savior *(John 3:16; 14:6)*. It is hard to understand this, but we will not be saddened by the lack of their presence. Our focus should not be on how we can enjoy heaven without all of our loved ones there, but on how we can point our loved ones to faith in Christ so that they will be there.

Hell is perhaps a primary reason why God sent Jesus Christ to pay the penalty for our sins. Being "extinguished" after death is no fate to dread, but an eternity in hell most definitely is. Jesus' death was an infinite death, paying our infinite sin debt so that we would not have to pay it in hell for eternity *(2 Corinthians 5:21)*. When we place our faith in Him, we are saved, forgiven, cleansed, and promised an eternal home in heaven. But if we reject God's gift of eternal life, we will face the eternal consequences of that decision.

14. Question: "Can people in heaven look down and see us?"

Hebrews 12:1 states, *"Therefore, since we are surrounded by such a great cloud of witnesses..."* Some understand the "cloud of witnesses" to be people looking down on us from heaven. That is not the correct interpretation. *Hebrews 11* records many people whom God commended for their faith. It is these people who are the "cloud of witnesses." They are "witnesses" not in that they are watching us, but rather in that they have set an example for us. They are witnesses for Christ and God and truth. *Hebrews 12:1* continues, *"...let us throw off everything that hinders and the sin that so easily entangles, and let us run with perseverance the race marked out for us."* Because of the faith and diligence of Christians who went before us, we should be inspired to follow their example.

The Bible does not specifically say whether or not people in heaven can look down on us who are still on the earth. It is highly unlikely that they can. Why? First, they would sometimes see things that would cause them grief or pain, namely, acts of sin and evil. Since there is no grief, tears, or unhappiness in heaven *(Revelation 21:4)*, it does not seem that observing earthly events would be possible. Second, people in heaven are so preoccupied with worshipping God and enjoying the glories of heaven that it does not seem they would have significant interest in what is happening here on earth. The very fact that they are free from sin and experiencing God's presence in heaven surely is more than enough to captivate their attention. While it is possible that God allows people in heaven to look down upon their loved ones, the Bible gives us no reason to believe this actually occurs.

15. Question: "What is the Judgment/Bema Seat of Christ?"

Romans 14:10-12 says, *"For we will all stand before God's judgment seat...so then, each of us will give an account of himself to God."* *2 Corinthians 5:10* tells us, *"For we must all appear before the judgment seat of Christ, that each one may receive what is due him for the things done while in the body, whether good or bad."* In the context, it is clear that both scriptures are referring to Christians, not unbelievers. The judgment seat of Christ, therefore, involves believers giving an account of their lives to Christ. The judgment seat of Christ does not determine salvation; that was determined by Christ's sacrifice on our behalf *(1 John 2:2)* and our faith in Him *(John 3:16)*. All of our sins are forgiven, and we will never be condemned for them *(Romans 8:1)*. We should not look at the judgment seat of Christ as God judging our sins, but rather as God rewarding us for our lives. Yes, as the Bible says, we will have to give an account of ourselves. Part of this is surely answering for the sins we committed. However, that is not going to be the primary focus of the judgment seat of Christ.

At the judgment seat of Christ, believers are rewarded based on how faithfully they served Christ *(1 Corinthians 9:4-27; 2 Timothy 2:5)*. Some of the things we might be judged on are how well we obeyed the Great Commission *(Matthew 28:18-20)*, how victorious we were over sin *(Romans 6:1-4)*, and how well we controlled our tongues *(James 3:1-9)*. The Bible speaks of believers receiving crowns for different things based on how faithfully they served Christ *(1 Corinthians 9:4-27; 2 Timothy 2:5)*. The various crowns are described in *2 Timothy 2:5, 2 Timothy 4:8, James 1:12, 1 Peter 5:4,* and *Revelation 2:10. James 1:12* is a good summary of how we should think about the judgment seat of Christ: *"Blessed is the man who perseveres under trial, because when he has stood the test, he will receive the crown of life that God has promised to those who love him."*

16. Question: "What is the Great White Throne Judgment?"

The great white throne judgment is described in *Revelation 20:11-15* and is the final judgment prior to the lost being cast into the lake of fire. We know from *Revelation 20:7-15* that this judgment will take place after the millennium and after Satan, the beast, and the false prophet are thrown into the lake of fire *(Revelation 20:7-10)*. The books that are opened *(Revelation 20:12)* contain records of everyone's deeds, whether they are good or evil, because God knows everything that has ever been said, done, or even thought, and He will reward or punish each one accordingly *(Psalm 28:4; 62:12; Romans 2:6; Revelation 2:23; 18:6; 22:12)*.

Also at this time, another book is opened, called the *"book of life" (Revelation 20:12)*. It is this book that determines whether a person will inherit eternal life with God or receive everlasting punishment in the lake of fire. Although Christians are held accountable for their actions, they are forgiven in Christ and their names were written in the *"book of life from the creation of the world" (Revelation 17:8)*. We also know from Scripture that it is at this judgment when the dead will be *"judged according to what they had done" (Revelation 20:12)* and that *"anyone's name"* that is not *"found written in the book of life"* will be *"thrown into the lake of fire" (Revelation 20:15)*.

The fact that there is going to be a final judgment for all men, both believers and unbelievers, is clearly confirmed in many passages of Scripture. Every person will one day stand before Christ and be judged for his or her deeds. While it is very clear that the great white throne judgment is the final judgment, Christians disagree on how it relates to the other judgments mentioned in the Bible, specifically, who will be judged at the great white throne judgment.

Some Christians believe that the Scriptures reveal three different judgments to come. The first is the judgment of the sheep and the goats or a judgment of the nations *(Matthew 25:31-36)*. This takes place after the tribulation period but prior to the millennium; its purpose is to determine who will enter the millennial kingdom. The second is a judgment of believers' works, often referred to as the *"judgment seat [bema] of Christ" (2 Corinthians 5:10)*. At this judgment, Christians will receive degrees of reward for their works or service to God. The third is the great white throne judgment at the end of the millennium *(Revelation 20:11-15)*. This is the judgment of unbelievers in which they are judged according to their works and sentenced to everlasting punishment in the lake of fire.

Other Christians believe that all three of these judgments speak of the same final judgment, not of three separate judgments. In other words, the great white throne judgment in *Revelation 20:11-15* will be the time that believers and unbelievers alike are judged. Those whose names are found in the book of life will be judged for their deeds in order to determine the rewards they will receive or lose. Those whose names are not in the book of life will be judged according to their deeds to determine the degree of punishment they will receive in the lake of fire. Those who hold this view believe that *Matthew 25:31-46* is another description of what takes place at the great white throne judgment. They point to the fact that the result of this judgment is the same as what is seen after the great white throne judgment in *Revelation 20:11-15*. The sheep (believers) enter into eternal life, while the goats (unbelievers) are cast into *"eternal punishment" (Matthew 25:46)*.

Whichever view one holds of the great white throne judgment, it is important to never lose sight of the facts concerning the coming judgment(s). First, Jesus Christ will be the judge, all unbelievers will be judged by Christ, and they will be punished according to the works they have done. The Bible is very clear that unbelievers are storing up wrath against themselves *(Romans 2:5)* and that God will *"give to each person according to what he has done" (Romans 2:6)*. Believers will also be judged by Christ, but since Christ's righteousness has been imputed to us and our names are written in the book of life, we will be rewarded, but not punished, according to our deeds. *Romans 14:10-12* says that we will all stand before the judgment seat of Christ and that each one of us will give an account to God.

17. Question: "Will there be marriage in heaven?"

The Bible tells us, *"At the resurrection people will neither marry nor be given in marriage; they will be like the angels in heaven" (Matthew 22:30)*. This was Jesus' answer in response to a question concerning a woman who had been married multiple times in her life —whom would she be married to in heaven *(Matthew 22:23-28)*? Evidently, there will be no such thing as marriage in heaven. This does not mean that a husband and wife will no longer know each other in heaven. This also does not mean that a husband and wife could not still have a close relationship in heaven. What it does seem to indicate, though, is that a husband and wife will no longer be married in heaven.

Most likely, there will be no marriage in heaven simply because there will be no need for it. When God established marriage, He did so to fill certain needs. First, He saw that Adam was in need of a companion. *"The LORD God said, 'It is not good for the man to be alone. I will make a helper suitable for him'" (Genesis 2:18)*. Eve was the solution to the problem of Adam's loneliness, as well as his need for a "helper," someone to come alongside him as his companion and go through life by his side. In heaven, however, there will be no loneliness, nor will there be any need for helpers. We will be surrounded by multitudes of believers and angels *(Revelation 7:9)*, and all our needs will be met, including the need for companionship.

Second, God created marriage as a means of procreation and the filling of the earth with human beings. Heaven, however, will not be populated by procreation. Those who go to heaven will get there by faith in the Lord Jesus Christ; they will not be created there by means of reproduction. Therefore, there is no purpose for marriage in heaven since there is no procreation or loneliness.

18. Question: "Will there be sex in heaven?"

In *Matthew 22*, the Sadducees, in an attempt to discredit Jesus, came to Him with a question regarding marriage and the resurrection. Jesus answered them with these words: *"At the resurrection people will neither marry nor be given in marriage; they will be like the angels in heaven" (verse 30)*. Jesus teaches here that marriage is a relationship to be enjoyed in this life, but it will not carry forward into the next life. While we do not lose our identity in heaven *(Luke 16:23)*, we will not hold the same relationships that we do on earth. Our existence will be quite different from what we are used to here. The fact that there is no marriage in heaven implies at least two other things:

>1) There will be no procreation in heaven; the number of the redeemed is set, and, with no death, there will be no need to propagate the race.
>2) There will be no sexual intercourse in heaven. The appetites and desires of this world will give way to higher and infi-

28

nitely more gratifying delights in the world to come.

For centuries, the temple and its sacrifices were at the heart of worship, but once Christ came and offered Himself as the ultimate sacrifice, the temple system and its sacrifices were no longer needed *(John 4:22-23)*. They were *"copies of the heavenly things,"* and the earthly temple was only *"a copy of the true one"* in heaven *(Hebrews 9:23-24)*. In the same way, the marriage relationship is a picture of our relationship with Christ *(Ephesians 5:31-32)*. Once we are present with Christ, the illustration will no longer be needed. We will have the reality, which is far better than any earthly representation. This is why Jesus is called the Bridegroom, the Church is called His Bride, and our celebration in heaven is called the Wedding *(John 3:29; Matthew 22:1-14; Revelation 19:7-9)*.

19. Question: "What does the Bible say about soul sleep?"

"Soul sleep" is a belief that after a person dies, his/her soul "sleeps" until the resurrection and final judgment. The concept of "soul sleep" is not biblical. When the Bible describes a person "sleeping" in relation to death *(Luke 8:52; 1 Corinthians 15:6)*, it does not mean literal sleep. Sleeping is just a way to describe death because a dead body appears to be asleep. The moment we die, we face the judgment of God *(Hebrews 9:27)*. For believers, to be absent from the body is to be present with the Lord *(2 Corinthians 5:6-8; Philippians 1:23)*. For unbelievers, death means everlasting punishment in hell *(Luke 16:22-23)*.

However, until the final resurrection there is a temporary heaven, paradise *(Luke 23:43; 2 Corinthians 12:4)* and a temporary hell, Hades *(Revelation 1:18; 20:13-14)*. As can be clearly seen in *Luke 16:19-31*, neither in paradise nor in Hades are people sleeping. It could be said, though, that a person's body is "sleeping" while his soul is in paradise or Hades. At the resurrection, this body is "awakened" and transformed into the everlasting body a person will possess for eternity, whether in heaven or hell. Those who were in paradise will be sent to the new heavens and new earth *(Revelation 21:1)*. Those who were in Hades will be thrown into the lake of fire *(Revelation 20:11-15)*. These are the final, eternal destinations of all people, based entirely on whether or not a person trusted in Jesus Christ for salvation.

Present-day defenders of soul sleep include the Seventh Day Adventist church, Jehovah's Witnesses, Christadelphians, and others.

20. Question: "What does the Bible say about when God will judge us?"

There are two separate judgments. Believers are judged at the Judgment Seat of Christ *(Romans 14:10-12)*. Every believer will give an account of himself, and the Lord will judge the decisions he made, including those concerning issues of conscience. This judgment does not determine salvation, which is by faith alone *(Ephesians 2:8-9)*, but rather is the time when believers must give an account of their lives in service to Christ. Our position in Christ is the "foundation" spoken of in *1 Corinthians 3:11-15*. That which we build upon the foundation can be the "gold, silver, and precious stones" of good works in Christ's name, obedience and fruitfulness, dedicated spiritual service to glorify God and build the church. Or what we build on the foundation may be the "wood, hay and stubble" of worthless, frivolous, shallow activity with no spiritual value. The Judgment Seat of Christ will reveal this.

The gold, silver and precious stones in the lives of believers will survive God's refining fire *(v. 13)*, and believers will be rewarded based on those good works, how faithfully we served Christ *(1 Corinthians 9:4-27)*, how well we obeyed the Great Commission *(Matthew 28:18-20)*, how victorious we were over sin *(Romans 6:1-4)*, how well we controlled our tongues *(James 3:1-9)*, etc. We will have to give an account for our actions, whether they were truly indicative of our position in Christ. The fire of God's judgment will completely burn up the "wood, hay and stubble" of the words we spoke and things we did which had no eternal value. *"So then, each of us will give an account of himself to God" (Romans 14:12)*.

The second judgment is that of unbelievers who will be judged at the Great White Throne Judgment *(Revelation 20:11-15)*. This judgment does not determine salvation, either. Everyone at the Great White Throne is an unbeliever who has rejected Christ in life and is therefore already doomed to the lake of fire. *Revelation 20:12* says that unbelievers will be *"judged out of those things which were written in the books, according to their works."* Those who have rejected Christ as Lord and Savior will be judged based on their works alone, and because the Bible tells us that *"by the works of the Law no flesh will be justified" (Galatians 2:16)*, they will be condemned. No amount of good works and the keeping of God's laws can be sufficient to atone for sin. All their thoughts, words and actions will be judged against God's perfect standard and found wanting. There will be no reward for them, only eternal condemnation and punishment.

21. Question: "How can Heaven be perfect if all of our loved ones are not there?"

It's hard to imagine that we can be happy in heaven if we have an awareness that those we loved on earth are not present. We do know that when we arrive in Heaven, we will not have anything to be saddened by. *Revelation 21:4* tells us, *"He will wipe every tear from their eyes. There will be no more death or mourning or crying or pain, for the old order of things has passed away."* Missing our loved ones would presumably fall under the category of pain or mourning. Perhaps we will have no knowledge or remembrance of them at all. Perhaps we will have come to see things from a heavenly perspective and will understand why our loved ones not being there somehow glorifies God and will rejoice. We do know that we will finally see everything from God's perspective, something which is impossible now. *"Now all we can see of God is like a cloudy picture in a mirror. Later we will see him face to face. We don't know everything, but then we will, just as God completely understands us" (1 Corinthians 13:12 CEV)*. In the meantime, we must accept by faith that what He says about Heaven is true and that we will have only joy for all eternity.

For a detailed description of Heaven, see *Revelations 21 & 22*. Once we arrive in Heaven, we will be glorified and perfect. Our hearts, attitudes, and thoughts will be completely in agreement with God *(1 John 3:2)*. If some of our loved ones are not in Heaven, we will be in 100% complete agreement that they do not belong ther, that they are condemned by their own refusal to accept Jesus Christ as their Savior *(John 3:16; John 14:6)*. It is hard to understand this, but we will not be saddened by the lack of their presence. Our focus should not be on how we can enjoy Heaven without all of our loved ones there, but rather on how we can point our loved ones to faith in Christ, so that they will be there.

22. Question: "How is eternity in hell a fair punishment for sin?"

This is an issue that bothers many people who have an incomplete understanding of three things: the nature of God, the nature of man, and the nature of sin. As fallen, sinful human beings, the nature of God is a difficult concept for us to grasp. We tend to see God as a kind, merciful Being whose love for us overrides and overshadows all His other attributes. Of course God is loving, kind, and merciful, but He is first and foremost a holy and righteous God. So holy is He that He cannot tolerate sin. He is a God whose anger burns against the wicked and disobedient *(Isaiah 5:25; Hosea 8:5; Zechariah 10:3)*. He is not only a loving God - He is love itself! But the Bible also tells us that He hates all manner of sin *(Proverbs 6:16-19)*. And while He is merciful, there are limits to His mercy. *"Seek the LORD while he may be found; call on him while he is near. Let the wicked forsake his way and the evil man his thoughts. Let him turn to the LORD, and he will have mercy on him, and to our God, for he will freely pardon" (Isaiah 55:6-7)*.

Humanity is corrupted by sin, and that sin is always directly against God. When David sinned by committing adultery with Bathsheba and having Uriah murdered, he responded with an interesting prayer: *"Against you, you only, have I sinned and done what is evil in your sight..." (Psalm 51:4)*. Since David had sinned against Bathsheba and Uriah, how could he claim to have only sinned against God? David understood that all sin is ultimately against God. God is an eternal and infinite being *(Psalm 90:2)*. As a result, all sin requires an eternal punishment. God's holy, perfect, and infinite character has been offended by our sin. Although to our finite minds our sin is limited in time, to God, who is outside of time, the sin He hates goes on and on. Our sin is eternally before Him and must be eternally punished in order to satisfy His holy justice.

No one understands this better than someone in hell. A perfect example is the story of the rich man and Lazarus. Both died, and the rich man went to hell while Lazarus went to paradise *(Luke 16)*. Of course, the rich man was aware that his sins were only committed during his lifetime. But, interestingly, he never says, "How did I end up here?" That question is never asked in hell. He does not say, "Did I really deserve this? Don't you think this is a little extreme? A little over the top?" He only asks that someone go to his brothers who are still alive and warn them against his fate.

Like the rich man, every sinner in hell has a full realization that he deserves to be there. Each sinner has a fully informed, acutely aware, and sensitive conscience which, in hell, becomes his own tormenter. This is the experience of torture in hell, a person fully aware of his or her sin with a relentlessly accusing conscience, without relief for even one moment. The guilt of sin will produce shame and everlasting self-hatred. The rich man knew that eternal punishment for a lifetime of sins is justified and deserved. That is why he never protested or questioned being in hell.

The realities of eternal damnation, eternal hell, and eternal punishment are frightening and disturbing. But it is good that we might, indeed, be terrified. While this may sound grim, there is good news. God loves us *(John 3:16)* and wants us to be saved from hell *(2 Peter 3:9)*. But because God is also just and righteous, He cannot allow our sin to go unpunished. Someone has to pay for it. In His great mercy and love, God provided His own payment for our sin. He sent His Son Jesus Christ to pay the penalty for our sins by dying on the cross for us. Jesus' death was an infinite death because He is the infinite God/man, paying our infinite sin debt, so that we would not have to pay it in hell for eternity *(2 Corinthians 5:21)*. If we confess our sin and place our faith in Christ, asking for God's forgiveness based on Christ's sacrifice, we are saved, forgiven, cleansed, and promised an eternal home in heaven. God loved us so much that He provided the means for our salvation, but if we reject His gift of eternal life, we will face the eternal consequences of that decision.

23. Question: "Where did Old Testament believers go when they died?"

The Old Testament teaches life after death, and that all people went to a place of conscious existence called Sheol. The wicked were there *(Psalm 9:17; 31:17; 49:14; Isaiah 5:14)*, and so were the righteous *(Genesis 37:35; Job 14:13; Psalm 6:5; 16:10; 88:3; Isaiah 38:10)*.

The New Testament equivalent of Sheol is Hades. Prior to Christ's resurrection, *Luke 16:19-31* shows Hades to be divided into two realms: a place of comfort where Lazarus was and a place of torment where the rich man was. The word hell in *verse 23* is not "Gehenna" (place of eternal torment) but "Hades" (place of the dead). Lazarus's place of comfort is elsewhere called Paradise *(Luke 23:43)*. Between these two districts of Hades is "a great gulf fixed" *(Luke 16:26)*.

Jesus is described as having descended into Hades after His death *(Acts 2:27, 31; cf. Ephesians 4:9)*. At the resurrection of Jesus Christ, it seems that the believers in Hades *(i.e., the occupants of Paradise)* were moved to another location. Now, Paradise is above rather than below *(2 Corinthians 12:2-4)*.

Today, when a believer dies, he is "present with the Lord" *(2 Corinthians 5:6-9)*. When an unbeliever dies, he follows the Old Testament unbelievers to Hades. At the final judgment, Hades will be emptied before the Great White Throne, where its occupants will be judged prior to entering the lake of fire *(Revelation 20:13-15)*.

24. Question: "Are there different levels of punishment in hell?"

The idea that there are different levels of punishment in hell derives primarily from the "Divine Comedy" written by Dante Alighieri between 1308 and 1321. In it, the Roman poet Virgil guides Dante through the nine circles of hell. The circles are concentric, representing a gradual increase in wickedness, and culminating at the center of the earth, where Satan is held in bondage. Each circle's sinners are punished in a fashion befitting their crimes. Each sinner is afflicted for all of eternity by the chief sin he committed. According to Dante, the circles range from the first circle, where dwell the unbaptized and virtuous pagans, to the very center of hell reserved for those who have committed the ultimate sin, treachery against God.

Although it does not specifically say so, the Bible might seem to indicate that there are different levels of punishment in hell. In *Revelation 20:11-15*, the people are judged *"according to what they had done as recorded in the books" (Revelation 20:12)*. All the people at this judgment, though, are thrown into the lake of fire *(Revelation 20:13-15)*. So, perhaps, the purpose of the judgment is to determine how severe the punishment in hell will be. Whatever the case, being thrown into a slightly less hot portion of the lake of fire is no consolation to those who are still doomed for eternity. Whatever degrees of punishment hell contains, it is clear that hell is a place to be avoided.

Unfortunately, the Bible states that most people will wind up in hell. *"...For wide is the gate and broad is the road that leads to destruction, and many enter through it. But small is the gate and narrow the road that leads to life, and only a few find it" (Matthew 7:13-14)*. The question one must ask is "which road am I on?" The "many" on the broad road have one thing in common—they have all rejected Christ as the one and only way to heaven. Jesus said, *"I am the way and the truth and the life. No one comes to the Father except through me" (John 14:6)*. When He said He is the only way, that is precisely what He meant. Everyone following another "way" beside Jesus Christ is on the broad road to destruction, and whether or not there are different levels of punishment in hell, the suffering is hideous, dreadful, eternal, and avoidable.

25. Question: "What is paradise? Is it different than Heaven?"

The word *paradise* is used as a synonym for "heaven" *(2 Corinthians 12:4; Revelation 2:7)*. When Jesus was dying on the cross and one of the thieves being crucified with Him asked Him for mercy, Jesus replied, *"I tell you the truth, today you will be with me in paradise" (Luke 23:43)*. Jesus knew that His death was imminent and that He would soon be in heaven with His Father. Therefore, Jesus used "paradise" as a synonym for "heaven."

What we do know for sure is that there has always been a separation of believers and unbelievers *(Luke 16:19-31)*. The righteous have always gone to paradise; the wicked have always gone to hell (hades). For right now, both heaven (paradise) and hell (Sheol) are "temporary holding places" until the day when Jesus Christ comes back to judge the world based on whether or not they have believed in Him. The first resurrection is of believers who will stand before the Judgment Seat of Christ to receive rewards based on meritorious service to Him. The second resurrection will be that of unbelievers who will stand before the Great White Throne Judgment of God. At this point, all will be sent to their eternal destination, the wicked to the lake of fire *(Revelation 20:11-15)*, and the righteous to a new heaven and a new earth *(Revelation 21-22)*.

26. Question: "What will we look like in Heaven?"

In the book of *1 Corinthians 15*, Paul talks about the resurrection and the resurrected body. In verses 35 and following, he states that our heavenly bodies will be different from our natural bodies, with some stark contrasts. Whereas our earthly bodies are characterized by mortality (being susceptible to death), our resurrected bodies will be characterized by immortality (not susceptible to death). Likewise, while our earthly bodies are susceptible to decay (corruption), they will become incorruptible *(1 Corinthians 15:53)*. Also, where our natural bodies are prone to weakness (ask anyone who has reached 40 years of age or older), our resurrected bodies will be characterized by strength *(verse 43)*.

Another comparison is that now we have a natural body, but then we will have a spiritual body. This probably doesn't mean that we will be like ghosts possessing no body at all and floating around unable to interact with things around us. After all, verse 49 states that we will have a body like Jesus' resurrected body (see also *1 John 3:2*). And Jesus, after His resurrection, told them to touch Him and to watch Him eat, demonstrating that He was not merely a spirit *(Luke 24:37-43)*. Rather, it's more likely that just as a natural body is fitted for this present life in our physical universe, the spiritual body will be that which will best suits us for the eternal existence we are destined for in our eternal abode. Jesus' resurrected body was capable of entering locked rooms at will *(John 20:19)*. Our earthly body limits us in ways (and/or dimensions) that our spiritual body will not.

1 Corinthians 15:43 also describes the transformation from *"sown in dishonor"* to *"raised in glory." Philippians 3:21* says that Jesus *"will transform our lowly body that it may be conformed to His glorious body."* Our decaying bodies are described with the word "dishonor" because they bear the mark of the results of sin. We can all picture the lungs of one who has ruined his health through smoking, or a brain that is no longer able to form complete thoughts because of drug abuse. In the same way, the decaying physical body is the direct result of man's sinfulness. Had there been no sin, there would be no decay and death *(1 Corinthians 15:56)*. But God, through Christ's transforming power, is able to raise up His children in Christ with new glorious bodies, being completely free from the ravages of sin and possessing the glory of Christ instead.

To summarize, we are not told exactly what we will look like in the next life, what age we will appear to be, or if we will look thin or fat. But, while many believe we will bear some resemblance to what we look like now, we do know that in whatever ways our appearance or health has been altered as a result of sin (whether because of overeating or not eating right, hereditary malformations, injuries, aging, etc.), these traits will not be carried over into our appearance in the next life. More importantly, the sin nature, inherited from Adam *(Romans 5:12)* will no longer be with us, for we will be made after the holiness of Christ *(1 John 3:2)*.

27. Question: "What does the Bible say about Purgatory?"

According to the Catholic Encyclopedia, Purgatory is "a place or condition of temporal punishment for those who, departing this life in God's grace, are not entirely free from venial faults, or have not fully paid the satisfaction due to their transgressions." To summarize, in Catholic theology Purgatory is a place that a Christian's soul goes to after death to be cleansed of the sins that had not been fully satisfied during life. Is this doctrine of Purgatory in agreement with the Bible? Absolutely not!

Jesus died to pay the penalty for all of our sins *(Romans 5:8)*. Isaiah 53:5 declares, *"But He was pierced for our transgressions, He was crushed for our iniquities; the punishment that brought us peace was upon Him, and by His wounds we are healed."* Jesus suffered for our sins so that we could be delivered from suffering. To say that we must also suffer for our sins is to say that Jesus' suffering was insufficient. To say that we must atone for our sins by cleansing in Purgatory is to deny the sufficiency of the atoning sacrifice of Jesus *(1 John 2:2)*. The idea that we have to suffer for our sins after death is contrary to everything the Bible says about salvation.

The primary Scriptural passage Catholics point to for evidence of Purgatory is *1 Corinthians 3:15*, which says, *"If it is burned up, he will suffer loss; he himself will be saved, but only as one escaping through the flames."* The passage *(1 Corinthians 3:12-15)* is using an illustration of things going through fire as a description of believers' works being judged. If our works are of good quality "gold, silver, costly stones," they will pass through the fire unharmed, and we will be rewarded for them. If our works are of poor quality "wood, hay, and straw," they will be consumed by the fire, and there will be no reward. The passage does not say that believers pass through the fire, but rather that a believer's works pass through the fire. *1 Corinthians 3:15* refers to the believer *"escaping through the flames,"* not *"being cleansed by the flames."*

Purgatory, like many other Catholic dogmas, is based on a misunderstanding of the nature of Christ's sacrifice. Catholics view the Mass/Eucharist as a re-presentation of Christ's sacrifice because they fail to understand that Jesus' once-for-all sacrifice was absolutely and perfectly sufficient *(Hebrews 7:27)*. Catholics view meritorious works as contributing to salvation due to a failure to recognize that Jesus' sacrificial payment has no need of additional "contribution" *(Ephesians 2:8 -9)*. Similarly, Purgatory is understood by Catholics as a place of cleansing in preparation for heaven because they do not recognize that because of Jesus' sacrifice, we are already cleansed, declared righteous, forgiven, redeemed, reconciled, and sanctified.

The very idea of Purgatory and the doctrines that are often attached to it (prayer for the dead, indulgences, meritorious works on behalf of the dead, etc.) all fail to recognize that Jesus' death was sufficient to pay the penalty for ALL of our sins. Jesus, who was God incarnate *(John 1:1,14)*, paid an infinite price for our sin. Jesus died for our sins *(1 Corinthians 15:3)*. Jesus is the atoning sacrifice for our sins *(1 John 2:2)*. To limit Jesus' sacrifice to atoning for original sin, or sins committed before salvation, is an attack on the Person and Work of Jesus Christ. If we must in any sense pay for, atone for, or suffer because of our sins, that indicates Jesus' death was not a perfect, complete, and sufficient sacrifice.

For believers, after death is to be *"away from the body and at home with the Lord" (2 Corinthians 5:6-8; Philippians 1:23)*. Notice that this does not say "away from the body, in Purgatory with the cleansing fire." No, because of the perfection, completion, and sufficiency of Jesus' sacrifice, we are immediately in the Lord's presence after death, fully cleansed, free from sin, glorified, perfected, and ultimately sanctified.

28. Question: "What does the Bible say about Limbo?"

The root of the word <u>limbo</u> is "the edge of a hem on a garment," so the word itself is telling us that limbo is someplace which borders very close to another. A very broad definition of <u>limbo</u> is "a zone which exists between two definite places." The Bible does not give the name "limbo" to any specific place or realm, but various people have used the word "limbo" in various ways.

One Roman Catholic tradition names a limbo for children who die before their baptisms or die outside of the Roman Catholic religion. There is no biblical support for this view. It is merely a religious opinion which has been handed down by Catholic theologians. For a study on the destiny of children who die, please read our article on the age of accountability.

The closest biblical account for a "limbo" concerns "Abraham's bosom" and "paradise" in the parable of the rich man and Lazarus *(Luke 16:19-31)*. Although it is a parable to teach a truth concerning prophecies declaring the kingdom of God, the places mentioned must exist or Jesus would not have used them. Parables are not based upon imaginary objects and locations, but on things which are real. So before the death and resurrection of Jesus Christ, there were two places souls went upon death. One place is at the side of Abraham (often described as Abraham's bosom); this would be for people who died in faith in God's promised Messiah, just as Abraham did, and were declared righteous by faith *(Genesis 15:4-6; Romans 4:13-24)*. Those who died in unbelief went to a place of torment. The Greek word used is *hades* and probably is the best Greek word for the Jewish *sheol*, literally "the lowest pit." It is clearly a place of great torment.

But this is also a temporary limbo. These souls will appear at the second resurrection before the great white throne of *Revelation 20:11-13*. These people are not in the Book of Life because they do not have eternal life through faith in Christ, and they are cast into their final destination in the "Lake of Fire/Gehenna." The idea of limbo as a realm in between heaven and hell, sort of another purgatory, is not biblical. If there is any sort of a limbo, it is the temporary holding place of the wicked (Hades / Sheol), which will eventually be emptied into the lake of fire *(Revelation 20:11-15)*.

29. Question: "What does the Bible say about reincarnation?"

The concept of reincarnation is completely without foundation in the Bible, which clearly tells us that we die once and then face judgment *(Hebrews 9:27)*. The Bible never mentions people having a second chance at life or coming back as different people or animals. Jesus told the criminal on the cross, *"Today you will be with me in paradise" (Luke 23:43)*, not "You will have another chance to live a life on this earth." *Matthew 25:46* specifically tells us that believers go on to eternal life while unbelievers go onto eternal punishment. Reincarnation has been a popular belief for thousands of years, but it has never been accepted by Christians or followers of Judaism because it is contradictory to Scripture.

The one passage that some point to as evidence for reincarnation is *Matthew 17:10-12* which links John the Baptist with Elijah. However, the passage does not say that John the Baptist was Elijah reincarnated but that he would have fulfilled the prophecy of Elijah's coming if the people had believed his words and thereby believed in Jesus as the Messiah *(Matthew 17:12)*. The people specifically asked John the Baptist if he was Elijah, and he said, *"No, I am not" (John 1:21)*.

Belief in reincarnation is an ancient phenomenon and is a central tenet within the majority of Indian religious traditions, such as Hinduism, Sikhism, and Jainism. Many modern pagans also believe in reincarnation as do some New Age movements, along with followers of spiritism. For the Christian, however, there can be no doubt: reincarnation is unbiblical and must be rejected as false.

30. Question: "How do I find comfort and peace when I have lost a loved one to death?"

Losing a loved one to death is a painful experience. Jesus understood the pain of losing someone close to His heart. In the *Book of John (11:1-44)*, we learn that Jesus lost a friend named Lazarus. Jesus was deeply moved and wept at the loss of His friend. This story, however, doesn't end in tears. Jesus knew He possessed the power needed to raise Lazarus from the dead. Jesus said, *"I am the resurrection and the life. He who believes in me will live even though he dies; and whoever lives and believes in me will never die" (John 11:25)*. Jesus overcame death through His resurrection. It is comforting to know that death is not the end for those who believe. Those who know Jesus as Savior will have eternal life *(John 10:28)*. God has prepared a new home for us where there will be no more death, tears or pain *(Revelation 21:1-4)*.

While you are healing from the loss of a loved one, God will comfort you *(2 Corinthians 7:6)*. The Bible tells us that God is the father of mercies and that He will comfort us in all our tribulations *(2 Corinthians 1:3-4)*. Be assured that God loves you and that He understands how much you are hurting. God promises you in *Isaiah 43:2* that when you go through deep waters and great trouble, He will be with you. When you go through rivers of difficulty, you will not drown. When you walk through the fire of oppression you will not be burned up; the flames will not consume you. Run to the shelter of the Most High where you will find sweet rest *(Psalm 91:1-2)*.

31. Question: "How should Christian parents handle the death of a child?"

As parents, we cannot imagine a more traumatic experience than losing a child. All parents naturally expect their children to outlive them. Such a loss is an extraordinary out-of-order event that brings with it an overwhelming sense of pain and lingering grief. It is a life-altering experience that presents unique challenges to parents as they seek to rebuild their lives without their child.

It would be presumptuous for anyone to tell parents how to handle the death of their child. However, we do know that those who yield their lives to God are more apt to recover from such a loss with a greater sense of normalcy than those without a genuine and positive faith in our Creator. With this being true, how do Christian parents handle the death of a child? Does the Bible address the subject, and if so, in what way?

First, we should note that each person handles grief differently. Emotions vary widely in their intensity. These emotions are normal and natural. Secondly, no parent ever "gets over" or "moves on" from the loss of a child. It's not like an illness from which we recover. Most counselors liken it to a life-changing physical injury. However, we should also know that though we may always feel the loss, its intensity does diminish with time.

It is the Christian's faith in a loving and ever-faithful God that enables us to endure and recover from the loss of a child, sometimes in ways that others find remarkable. Such was the case of David in the loss of his first child who died seven days after birth *(2 Samuel 12:18-19)*. There are several valuable lessons we can learn from this passage of Scripture that can help grieving parents to face the future with hope.

One is that David prayed fervently for his child's life *(2 Samuel 12:16)*. This should be true for all parents at all times, and not just when times are difficult. Parents should always pray for our children, asking God to watch over and protect them. Likewise, parents should pray that God provides godly wisdom and guidance so that our children grow in the nurture and admonition of the Lord *(Judges 13:12; Proverbs 22:6; Ephesians 6:4)*.

Another lesson we learn from David was his reaction to his child's death. Upon learning that the infant had died, there was an acceptance signified by His actions when he *"arose from the ground, washed and anointed himself, and changed his clothes; and he went into the house of the LORD and worshiped. Then he went to his own house; and when he requested, they set food before him, and he ate" (2 Samuel 12:20)*. What is surprising about this passage is that David *"went into the house of the Lord and worshiped."* In other words, David not only accepted the death of his child, but he gave it all over to God in worship. The ability to worship and honor God in a time of trial or crisis is a powerful demonstration of our spiritual confidence in our God. Doing so enables us to accept the reality of our loss. And this is how God frees us to go on living. What David models for us in this story is learning to turn loose what we cannot change.

The next lesson is the most revealing. It is confidence in the knowledge that children who die before they reach the age of accountability go to heaven. David's response to those questioning his reaction to the death of his child has always been a great source of comfort to believing parents who have lost infants and young children. *"But now that he is dead, why should I fast? Can I bring him back again? I will go to him, but he will not return to me" (2 Samuel 12:23)*. David was fully confident that he would meet his son in heaven. This passage is a powerful indication that babies as well as children who pass from this world will go to heaven.

Grieving the loss of a child is a heartrending journey. There are no hard and fast rules or guidelines to teach us how to handle our mourning. However, counselors and those who have experienced the loss of a child have provided some helpful advice:

- Recognize that you are not alone. You have God. You have your brothers and sisters in Christ. You have close friends and family. Lean on them. They are there to help you.
- Don't put time limits on your recovery. Don't expect a day to pass without thinking about your child, nor should you want to.
- Talk about your child. It's important that you share the story of your child with others.
- Take care of yourself and your other children. They, too, are suffering loss of a sibling and the additional discomfort of seeing their parents in grief.
- Try not to make any major decisions at least for the first year.
- Expect that getting through the many "firsts" following the death of a young child (first birthday, first Christmas, etc) will be painful.
- And lastly, Christians who have lost a child have the grand and faithful promise of God's word: *"And God shall wipe away all tears from their eyes; and there shall be no more death, neither sorrow, nor crying, neither shall there be any more pain: for the former things are passed away" (Revelation 21:4).*

32. Question: "How can I find comfort when an unsaved loved one has died?"

For the believer, the death of an unsaved loved one is very difficult. Sometimes it seems we will never find comfort or peace of mind when we know the destiny awaiting the unsaved. When a saved loved one dies, we miss him, but we do not grieve *"as others who have no hope" (1 Thessalonians 4:13),* because we know we will be reunited in heaven one day.

But for those who die without Christ, we know we will not see them again and finding comfort in that situation is very painful.

Especially for those who have taken great pains to communicate Gospel truths to their loved ones, there is associated with this situation a pain that asks "why?" As Christians, we wonder how anyone could refuse such a precious gift. Our joy in the Lord moves us to want that same joy for others. However, the truth is that even though the invitation is open to all, some will not receive the gift. But we can take comfort, encouragement, and assurance in the truth that even though we may never see our loved one again, God is always faithful and just. It is amazing to understand that God is so patient and leaves the door open for so long.

"Shall not the Judge of all the earth do right" (Genesis 18:25)? This is a great comfort to those of us with loved ones who have passed into eternity and we are not sure of the destination of their souls. God is a sovereign Judge of righteousness, full of grace and mercy to all who call upon Him. It is His very justice that offers a "way" for all to escape the judgment of His righteousness, and it is in that justice that we must rest. It is grace that saves us, and it is grace in which we must stand when we go through the double grief of the death of an unsaved loved one. We must remember that we cannot make this choice for anyone else, and if they went into eternity without Christ, that was their choice in spite of the offer of grace.

Although we may have pain in the remembrance of that loved one while we are in this life and go through the grief process, there will come a time when each born-again believer will be with the Lord. In that day *"God shall wipe away all tears from their eyes; and there shall be no more death, neither sorrow, nor crying, neither shall there be any more pain: for the former things are passed away" (Revelation 21:4)*. We cannot comprehend how that will be because we live in time and are constrained by our finite minds. However, just the thought of that is enough to bring comfort and encouragement. When we see the Lord, all of the sorrow we have now will disappear. *"You now have sorrow; but I will see you again and your heart will rejoice, and your joy no one will take from you" (John 16:22)*. In the meantime, we can lean on the everlasting arms of God, who feels our pain and comforts us with His great love and mercy.

33. Question: "What will we be doing in Heaven?"

In *Luke 23:43*, Jesus declared, *"Truly I say to you, today you shall be with me in paradise."* The word Jesus used for "paradise" is *paradeisos* which means "a park, that is, (specifically) an Eden (place of future happiness, paradise)". Paradeisos is the Greek word taken from the Hebrew word pardes which means "a park: - forest, orchard" (Strong's). Jesus said, "Today you shall be with me "en paradeisos," not "en nephele" which is Greek for "in clouds." The point is that Jesus picked and used the word for "a park." Not just any park but "the paradise of God" or park of God *(Revelation 2:7)* which for us will be a place of future happiness. Does this sound like a boring place? When you think of a park, do you think of boredom?

Jesus said, *"You shall worship the Lord your God, and Him only you shall serve" (Matthew 4:10).* It's interesting to note that Jesus did not say "praise and serve." Even the briefest examination of the word praise in the Bible quickly shows it's a verbal thing and is for the most part singing. Worship, however, is from the heart. Worship manifests itself in praise. Serving God is worship, and Scripture is clear we will serve God in heaven. *"His servants will serve Him" (Revelation 22:3).* We are unable to fully serve God in this life due to sin, but in heaven *"every curse will no longer be" (Revelation 22:3).* We will not be under the curse of sin any longer, so everything we do will be worship in heaven. We will never be motivated by anything other than our love for God. Everything we do will be out of our love for God, untainted by our sin nature.

So what will we do? My favorite thing is to learn. *"For who has known the mind of the Lord, or who became His counselor?" (Romans 11:34)*, *"In whom are hidden all the treasures of wisdom and knowledge" (Colossians 2:3).* God is the *"the high and lofty One who inhabits eternity" (Isaiah 57:15).* God is bigger than forever, and it will take eternity *"to comprehend with all saints what is the breadth and length and depth and height, and to know the love of Christ" (Ephesians 3:18-19).* In other words, we will never stop learning.

God's Word says we won't have to be in His paradise alone. *"I shall fully know even as I also am fully known" (1 Corinthians 13:12).* This would seem to indicate that we will not only know our friends and family, we will "fully know" them. In other words, there is no need for secrets in heaven. There is nothing to be ashamed of. There is nothing to hide. We will have eternity to interact with *"a great multitude, which no man could number, out of all nations and kindreds and people and tongues" (Revelation 7:9)*. No wonder heaven will be a place of infinite learning. Just getting to know everyone will take eternity!

Any further anticipation about what we shall do in God's eternal park, heaven, will be far surpassed when *"the King shall say to those on His right hand, 'Come, blessed of My Father, inherit the kingdom prepared for you from the foundation of the world'" (Matthew 25:34)*. Whatever we will be doing, we can be sure it will be wonderful beyond our imaginations!

34. Question: "What age will everyone be in Heaven?"

The Bible does not specifically answer this question. Will babies and children who die still be babies/children in Heaven? What about elderly people who die, do they remain elderly in heaven? Some have guessed that babies are given a resurrection body *(1 Corinthians 15:35 -49)* that is "fast-forwarded" to the "ideal age," just as those who die at an old age are "re-wound" to the ideal age. This would indicate that there won't be any children or elderly people in heaven.

What is the ideal age? Again, this concept is not specifically biblical. Some believe it to be around 30. Some guess 33 since that is approximately the age Jesus was when He died. *1 John 3:2* declares, *"Dear friends, now we are children of God, and what we will be has not yet been made known. But we know that when He appears, we shall be like Him, for we shall see Him as He is."*

One thing is for certain. Whatever age we appear to be, we will be gloriously perfect. Our entire person will be remade flawless, wholly and completely Christ-like. We will lose all trace of human fallenness, wearing the white robes of purity, holiness and absolute perfection. So whatever age we are, it will be the age of complete and total perfection.

35. Question: "Will we have physical bodies in Heaven?"

Although the Bible tells us little about what it will be like in heaven, it seems that we will most likely have a physical body, although not in the same sense of "physical" that we have now. *1 Corinthians 15:52* says that *"the dead will be raised incorruptible"* and that those who are alive at the time of Christ's return for His saints *"shall be changed."* Jesus Christ is *"the first fruits"* of those who have died *(1 Corinthians 15:20, 23)*. This means that He set the example and leads the way. *1 Corinthians 15:42* says that our *"body is sown in corruption, it is raised in incorruption."* In a precursor to the believers' resurrection, some were raised at the time of Christ's resurrection in *Matthew 27:52* where it says that their *"bodies...were raised."* Thomas, in *John 20:27*, physically touched the body of Christ following His resurrection, so He obviously had a body that was solid.

We can expect that all believers' resurrection will be like that of Christ's. What a wonderful truth! The Bible is not specific, but it seems that we will be able to eat. John, in *Revelation 22:2*, writes of his vision of the eternal state where he saw that *"in the middle of its street, and on either side of the river, was the tree of life, which bore twelve fruits, each tree yielding its fruit every month."* This seems to be a reversal of the *Genesis 3* punishment where Adam and Eve, and hence all of mankind, were banned from eating from this tree. As for hunger, it appears that there won't be any. *Isaiah 49:10* says that there will be no hunger or thirst in the millennial kingdom. This is speaking of mortal men during that period, not of translated saints, but by extension it can be said that if mortals on earth during Christ's Kingdom do not hunger, then surely there will be no hunger in heaven (see also *Revelation 7:14-16*).

Finally, Job wrote that he knew for sure that even after he dies and his skin is long gone, that *"in my FLESH I shall SEE God"* (*Job 19:25* all caps added for emphasis). So that means our bodies will consist of some kind of glorified flesh. Whatever form we have, we know that it will be perfect, sinless and flawless.

36. Question: "What does the Bible say about death?"

The Bible presents death as separation: physical death is the separation of the soul from the body, and spiritual death is the separation of the soul from God.

Death is the result of sin. *"For the wages of sin is death,"* Romans *6:23a.* The whole world is subject to death, because all have sinned. *"By one man sin entered the world, and death by sin, and so death passed upon all men, for that all have sinned" (Romans 5:12).* In *Genesis 2:17,* the Lord warned Adam that the penalty for disobedience would be death, *"you will surely die."* When Adam disobeyed, he experienced immediate spiritual death, which caused him to hide *"from Lord God among the trees of the garden" (Genesis 3:8).* Later, Adam experienced physical death *(Genesis 5:5).*

On the cross, Jesus also experienced physical death *(Matthew 27:50).* The difference is that Adam died because he was a sinner, and Jesus, who had never sinned, chose to die as a substitute for sinners *(Hebrews 2:9).* Jesus then showed His power over death and sin by rising from the dead on the third day *(Matthew 28; Revelation 1:18).* Because of Christ, death is a defeated foe. *"O death, where is thy sting? O grave, where is thy victory?" (1 Corinthians 15:55; Hosea 13:14).*

For the unsaved, death brings to an end the chance to accept God's gracious offer of salvation. *"It is appointed unto men once to die, but after this the judgment" (Hebrews 9:27).* For the saved, death ushers us into the presence of Christ: *"To be absent from the body, and to be present with the Lord" (2 Corinthians 5:8; Philippians 1:23).* So real is the promise of the believer's resurrection that the physical death of a Christian is called "sleep" *(1 Corinthians 15:51; 1 Thessalonians 5:10).* We look forward to that time when *"there shall be no more death" (Revelation 21:4).*

37. Question: "Do we have an appointed time of death?"

The Bible tells us that *"all the days ordained for me were written in your book before one of them came to be" (Psalm 139:16)*. So, yes, God knows exactly when, where, and how we will die. God knows absolutely everything about us *(Psalm 139:1-6)*. So does this mean our fate is sealed? Does this mean we have absolutely no control over when we will die? The answer is both yes and no, depending on the perspective.

The answer is "yes" from God's perspective because God is omniscient. He knows everything and knows exactly when, where and how we will die. Nothing we can do will change what God already knows will happen. The answer is "no" from our perspective because we do have an impact on when, where, and how we die. Obviously, a person who commits suicide causes his own death. A person who commits suicide would have lived longer had he not committed suicide. Similarly, a person who dies because of a foolish decision (e.g., drug use) "expedites" his own death. A person who dies of lung cancer from smoking would not have died in the same way or at the same time if he had not smoked. A person who dies of a heart attack due to a lifetime of extremely unhealthy eating and little exercise would not have died in the same way or at the same time if he had eaten healthier foods and exercised more. Yes, our own decisions have an undeniable impact on the manner, timing, and place of our death.

How does this affect our lives practically? We are to live each day for God. *James 4:13-15* teaches us, *"Now listen, you who say, 'Today or tomorrow we will go to this or that city, spend a year there, carry on business and make money.' Why, you do not even know what will happen tomorrow. What is your life? You are a mist that appears for a little while and then vanishes. Instead, you ought to say, 'If it is the Lord's will, we will live and do this or that.'"* We are to make wise decisions about how we live our lives and how we take care of ourselves. And ultimately, we trust God that He is sovereign and in control of all things.

38. Question: "What does the Bible say about near death experiences?"

There is no specific scriptural support for near-death experiences. Many people use *2 Corinthians 12:2-5* as a biblical proof text of near-death experiences. However, this is taking great liberty with interpretation and makes the assumption that Paul had actually died when he found himself in heaven. The passage nowhere states that Paul had died. It was a vision that God gave Paul of heaven, not a near-death experience.

We need to be extremely careful in how we validate our experiences. The most important test of any experience is comparing it with the Bible. Satan is always ready to cause deception and twist people's thinking. *"But I am not surprised! Even Satan can disguise himself as an angel of light. So it is no wonder his servants can also do it by pretending to be godly ministers. In the end they will get every bit of punishment their wicked deeds deserve" (2 Corinthians 11:14-15).* Because the Bible is silent regarding near-death experiences, and scientific research has not been able to be performed reliably, we simply cannot accept the legitimacy of near death experiences on their face value. It would be too strong to state that all near-death experiences are faked, imagined, or Satanic, but there are still serious concerns, biblically, about the validity of near-death experiences.

39. Question: "What is the first resurrection? What is the second resurrection?"

Daniel 12:2 summarizes the two very different fates facing mankind: *"Many of them that sleep in the dust of the earth shall awake, some to everlasting life, and some to shame and everlasting contempt."* Everyone will be raised from the dead, but not everyone will share the same destiny. The New Testament reveals the further detail of separate resurrections for the just and the unjust.

Revelation 20:4-6 mentions a "first resurrection" and identifies those involved as "blessed and holy." The second death (the lake of fire,

Revelation 20:14) has no power over these individuals. The first resurrection, then, is the raising of all believers. It corresponds with Jesus' teaching of the *"resurrection of the just" (Luke 14:14)* and the *"resurrection of life" (John 5:29)*.

The first resurrection takes place in various stages. Jesus Christ Himself (the *"first fruits," 1 Corinthians 15:20*), paved the way for the resurrection of all who believe in Him. There was a resurrection of the Jerusalem saints (*Matthew 27:52-53*) which should be included in our consideration of the first resurrection. Still to come are the resurrection of *"the dead in Christ"* at the Lord's return (*1 Thessalonians 4:16*) and the resurrection of the martyrs at the end of the Tribulation (*Revelation 20:4*).

Revelation 20:12-13 identifies those comprising the second resurrection as the wicked judged by God at the great white throne judgment prior to being cast into the lake of fire. The second resurrection, then, is the raising of all unbelievers; the second resurrection is connected to the second death. It corresponds with Jesus' teaching of the *"resurrection of damnation" (John 5:29)*.

The event which divides the first and second resurrections seems to be the millennial kingdom. The last of the righteous are raised to reign *"with Christ a thousand years" (Revelation 20:4)*, but the *"rest of the dead [that is, the wicked] lived not again until the thousand years were finished" (Revelation 20:5)*.

What great rejoicing will attend the first resurrection! What great anguish at the second! What a responsibility we have to share the Gospel! *"And others save with fear, pulling them out of the fire" (Jude 23)*.

40. Question: "Will we remember our earthly lives when we are in Heaven?"

Isaiah 65:17 tells us, *"For, behold, I create new heavens and a new earth: and the former shall not be remembered, nor come into mind."* Some interpret *Isaiah 65:17* as saying that we will have no memory of our earthly lives in heaven. However, one verse earlier in *Isaiah 65:16*, the Bible says, *"For the past troubles will be forgotten and hidden from my eyes."* It is likely only our "past troubles" that will be forgotten, not all of our memories. Our memories will be cleansed, redeemed, healed, and restored, not erased. There is no reason why we could not possess many memories from our earthly lives. The memories that will be cleansed are the ones that involve sin, pain, and sadness. *Revelation 21:4* declares, *"He will wipe every tear from their eyes. There will be no more death or mourning or crying or pain, for the old order of things has passed away."*

Some point to the story of Lazarus and the rich man *(Luke 16:19-31)* as proof that the dead remember their earthly lives. The rich man asked Abraham to send Lazarus back to earth to warn the rich man's brothers not to come to hell. So he remembered his relatives. He must have also remembered his own life of sin because he never asked to be released from hell, nor did he ask why he was there or claim there had been some kind of mistake. He remembered enough about his earthly life to know that he deserved hell. But this is no proof that those in heaven remember their earthly lives. The rich man's remembrance was part of his misery. If we have memories in heaven, they will only be of things that will bring us joy.

41. Question: "What are the New Heavens and the New Earth?"

Many people have a misconception of what heaven is truly like. *Revelation 21-22* gives us a detailed picture of the new heavens and the new earth. After the events of the end times, the current heavens and earth will be done away with and replaced by the new heavens and new earth. The eternal dwelling place of believers will be the new earth. The new earth is the "heaven" on which we will spend eternity. It is the new earth where the New Jerusalem, the heavenly city, will be located. It is on the new earth that the pearly gates and streets of gold will be.

Heaven, the new earth, is a physical place where we will dwell with glorified physical bodies *(1 Corinthians 15:35-58)*. The concept that heaven is "in the clouds" is unbiblical. The concept that we will be "spirits floating around in heaven" is also unbiblical. The heaven that believers will experience will be a new and perfect planet on which we will dwell. The new earth will be free from sin, evil, sickness, suffering, and death. It will likely be similar to our current earth, or perhaps even a re-creation of our current earth, but without the curse of sin.

What about the new heavens? It is important to remember that in the ancient mind, "heavens" referred to the skies and outer space, as well as the realm in which God dwells. So, when *Revelation 21:1* refers to the new heavens, it is likely indicating that the entire universe will be created, a new earth, new skies, new outer space. It seems as if God's heaven will be recreated as well, to give everything in the universe a "fresh start," whether physical or spiritual. Will we have access to the new heavens in eternity? Possibly, but we will have to wait to find out. May we all allow God's Word to shape our understanding of heaven.

42. Question: "Will it be possible for us to sin in Heaven?"

The Bible describes heaven in great detail in *Revelation 21-22*. Nowhere in those chapters is the possibility of sin mentioned. There will be no more death, sorrow, crying, or pain *(Revelation 21:4)*. The sinful are not in heaven, but in the lake of fire *(Revelation 21:8)*. Nothing impure will ever enter heaven *(Revelation 21:27)*. Outside of heaven are those who sin *(Revelation 22:15)*. So, the answer is no, there will be no sin in heaven.

What does that mean for us? If there is no possibility of sin, does that mean we will no longer have a free will in heaven? Perhaps in heaven, our ability to choose will be similar to that of the angels. The angels had a one-time choice to obey God or follow Satan. There is no possibility of further angels sinning and joining Satan in his rebellion. The holy angels are *"elect angels" (1 Timothy 5:21)*. Similarly, the elect in heaven will be "sealed" in their decision to forsake sin and trust in Christ. We will not even have the choice to sin. At the same time, having been delivered from sin and evil, and viewing the wonderful glories of heaven, we would not choose sin even if we had the choice.

43. Question: "Do we become angels after we die?"

Angels are beings created by God *(Colossians 1:15-17)* and are entirely different from humans. They are God's special agents to carry out His plan and to minister to the followers of Christ *(Hebrews 1:13-14)*. There is no indication that angels were formerly humans or anything else, they were created as angels. Angels have no need of, and cannot experience, the redemption that Christ came to provide for the human race. *1 Peter 1:12* describes their desire to look into the Gospel, but it is not for them to experience. Had they been formerly humans, the concept of salvation would not be a mystery to them, having experienced it themselves. Yes, they rejoice when a sinner turns to Christ *(Luke 15:10)*, but salvation in Christ is not for them.

Eventually, the body of the believer in Christ will die. What happens then? The spirit of the believer goes to be with Christ *(2 Corinthians 5:8)*. The believer does not become an angel. It is interesting that both Elijah and Moses were recognizable on the Mount of Transfiguration. They had not transformed into angels, but appeared as themselves, although glorified, and were recognizable to Peter, James and John.

In *1 Thessalonians 4:13-18*, Paul tells us that believers in Christ are asleep in Jesus; that is, their bodies are dead, but their spirits are alive. This text tells us that when Christ returns, He will bring with Him those who are asleep in Him, and then their bodies will be raised, made new like Christ's resurrected body, to be joined with their spirits which He brings with Him. All believers in Christ who are living at the return of Christ will have their bodies changed to be like Christ, and they will be completely new in their spirits, no longer having a sin nature.

All the believers in Christ will recognize one another and live with the Lord forever. We will serve Him throughout eternity, not as angels, but along with the angels. Thank the Lord for the living hope He provides for the believer in Jesus Christ.

44. Question: "Will there be such a thing as gender in Heaven?"

Matthew 22:30 speaks of people after the resurrection not participating in marriage, they become "like the angels." However, this does not mean people are genderless. The masculine, not neuter, pronoun is used many times to describe angels (and HE was like...HIS appearance was like, etc.). So there is no real indication that the angels are genderless beings.

There is nothing in the Bible that indicates people will lose or change their gender in heaven. In the book of *Revelation 21-22*, it seems that God is making things not just like they were in the Garden of Eden, but even better. Remember that gender is not bad, it is actually a good thing. God created Eve because Adam needed someone to complement him. Marriage (impossible without different genders), the model relationship between a man and a woman, is a picture of Christ and the church. The church is the bride and Christ is the groom *(Ephesians 5:25-32)*.

Although it is not explicitly taught in the Bible, it seems most likely that people retain their gender after death. Our genders are a part of who we are. Gender is more than physical, it is part of our very nature and part of the way we relate to God. Therefore, it seems that gender will be perfected and glorified in eternity. It is also noteworthy that Jesus retained His gender after His death and resurrection.

45. Question: "Why do so many people have to experience terrible suffering before death?"

Suffering is a universal part of our humanity that exists in a fallen world. The question of why there is suffering in death for some and not as much for others is really not answerable. For we reckon things from our human experience and do not understand the infinite mind and purpose of God. In the great faith chapter, we often read of the heroes of the faith but neglect the litany of those unnamed who suffered for their faith *(Hebrews 11:33-40)*. These all died suffering deaths yet are heroes of the faith. They are unnamed and unsung among men, but God values their suffering and includes them in this great chapter of faith as a lesson to us.

Suffering and death are part of the curse of sin on the world *(Genesis 3:16-19)*. Adam and Eve fell, and when they did, they brought to themselves and to all of their descendants the suffering of death. *"But you must not eat from the tree of the knowledge of good and evil, for when you eat of it you will surely die" (Genesis 2:17)*. We know that Adam and Eve did not die physically on the day that they ate of the tree. Adam lived to the age of 930 *(Genesis 5:5)*. But when Adam sinned, he was spiritually separated from God, and this is the first death.

The question of why some suffer at death and others do not could be summed up in one statement: "God is sovereign." That is not just a trite and easy statement. When Jesus healed a man born blind, the disciples questioned Him. *"'Rabbi, who sinned, this man or his parents, that he was born blind?' 'Neither this man nor his parents sinned,' said Jesus, 'but this happened so that the work of God might be displayed in his life'" (John 9:1-3)*. In this passage is a principle that can be applied to our question. God allows some to suffer so that *"the work of God might be displayed."* In other words, God allows some to suffer to bring glory to His name and others not to suffer for the same reason. It is His sovereign will that determines each circumstance. Therefore, we can safely say that no suffering is without a purpose in the plan of God, even though we as finite humans may not see that purpose clearly.

The Apostle Paul suffered much in his life and ministry. A litany of that suffering can be found in *2 Corinthians 11:23-27*. Paul was killed for his testimony and according to universal tradition was decapitated after a long imprisonment. However, during this time, he wrote this testimony to Timothy: *"I have fought the good fight, I have finished the race, I have kept the faith. Now there is in store for me the crown of righteousness, which the Lord, the righteous Judge, will award to me on that day, and not only to me, but also to all who have longed for his appearing" (2 Timothy 4:7-8)*. Another purpose for suffering is to be a witness to those watching that God's grace and strength is sufficient to enable a believer to stand in that suffering *(2 Corinthians 12:9)*.

Paul also gives us an example as to how we should view suffering as a child of God. *"But he said to me, 'My grace is sufficient for you, for my power is made perfect in weakness.' Therefore I will boast all the more* gladly about my weaknesses, so that Christ's power may rest on me. That is why, for Christ's sake, I delight in weaknesses, in insults, in hardships, in persecutions, in difficulties. For when I am weak, then I am strong" (2 Corinthians 12:9-10). And Paul also said, "For me to live is Christ, to die is gain" (Philippians 1:21). Therefore, however a believer dies, in suffering or in relative peace, it is but a transition to "face to face" with the LORD. Once that transition has been made, all of the sorrow and pain of the suffering will end. "He will wipe every tear from their eyes. There will be no more death or mourning or crying or pain, for the old order of things has passed away" (Revelation 21:4).

46. Question: "What is the New Jerusalem?"

The New Jerusalem, which has also been called the Tabernacle of God, the Holy City, the City of God, the Celestial City, and Heavenly Jerusalem, is literally heaven on earth. It is referred to in the Bible in several places (Isaiah 52:1, Galatians 4:26, Hebrews 11:10, 12:22-24, and 13:14), but it is most fully described in the 21st chapter of the book of Revelation.

The Bible is a unique, supernatural book, and while what we see in nature and the physical universe is God's natural revelation to man (Romans 1:19-20), the Bible is God's special revelation to man (2 Timothy 3:16 and 2 Peter 1:20). It tells us of the creation of our universe and of the creation of man. It tells of man's falling away from God and the sin nature that we all inherit because of that fall (Romans 3:23). It also tells of God's plan for man's redemption through the person of Jesus Christ, God incarnate (John 3:16).

However, the Bible is much, much more than that. The Bible teaches us how we should live through various examples of the recorded history of the Jewish people, God's chosen people. This is exemplified through seven different dispensations of time. In each one of these dispensations, man is given a responsibility, and in each one man fails. This is God's way of showing us just how hopelessly lost we really are.

The Bible is the manual of life for the Christian, and it is the only sacred writing of any of the world's religions that proves itself by its predictive prophecy. But it is not a book for everyone. Admittedly, while everyone can profit from the wisdom contained in the Bible, only the Christian, or rather the "born-again" believer (see *John 3:3)*, will truly profit from the Bible (see *1 Corinthians 2:14, Ephesians 1:13-14*, and *John 16:13)*.

But, by the time we reach the *21st chapter of Revelation*, the recorded history of man is at its end. All of the ages have come and gone. Christ has gathered His church in the Rapture *(1 Thessalonians 4:15-17)*. The Tribulation and the Great Tribulation of the book of Revelation have past. The battle of Armageddon has been fought and won by our Lord Jesus Christ *(Revelation 19:17-21)*. Satan has been chained for the thousand-year reign of Christ on earth; he was released and deceived the nations once again, causing them to rise up in rebellion against God once more, but God has defeated Satan again and Satan has received his just punishment, an eternity in the lake of fire *(Revelation 20:1-10.)* The Great White Throne Judgment has taken place, and mankind has been judged *(Revelation 20:11-15)*.

Now in *Revelation 21* the new heaven and the new earth have come, God the Father then brings heaven to earth in the New Jerusalem where He dwells with His own for eternity. Only God's children will be with Him in the New Jerusalem *(John 1:12)*. Do you belong to Him? In *Ecclesiastes* Solomon tells us of the futility of our pursuits in this life. *Verse 3:11* tells us that since we were made for eternity nothing in time will fully and permanently satisfy us. Aquinas wrote, *"You have made us for yourself, O Lord, and we are restless until we find our rest in you."*

The New Jerusalem is where believers in Christ will spend eternity. The New Jerusalem is the ultimate fulfillment of all God's promises. The New Jerusalem is heaven, paradise, God's goodness made fully manifest. Have you accepted God's invitation to the New Jerusalem? If not, or if you are not sure, please visit http://www.gotquestions.org/eternal-life.html. If you have accepted God's invitation to the New Jerusalem, I look forward to seeing you there!

47. Question: "Is the Divine Comedy/Dante's Inferno a biblically accurate description of Heaven and Hell?"

Written by Dante Alighieri between 1308 and 1321, the Divine Comedy is widely considered the central epic poem of Italian literature. A brilliantly written allegory, filled with symbolism and pathos, it is certainly one of the classics of all time. The poem is written in the first person in which Dante describes his imaginative journey through the three realms of the dead: "Inferno" (hell); "Purgatorio" (Purgatory); and "Paradiso" (heaven).

The philosophy of the poem is a mixture of the Bible, medieval Roman Catholicism, mythology, and Middle Ages tradition. Where Dante draws on his knowledge of the Bible, the poem is truthful and insightful. Where he draws on the other sources, the poem departs from truth. In fairness to Dante, however, it should be noted that his work is intended to be literary, not theological. It does reflect a deep yearning for understanding of the mysteries of life and death and, as such, has generated tremendous interest over the centuries, remaining extremely popular even today.

When comparing the poem to the Bible, many differences surface. Apparent immediately is the third of the work devoted to Purgatory, a doctrine of the Roman Catholic Church having no foundation in the Bible. In Dante's poem, the Roman poet Virgil guides Dante through the seven terraces of Purgatory. These correspond to the seven deadly sins, each terrace purging a particular sin until the sinner has corrected the nature within himself that caused him to commit that sin, thus enabling him to proceed at some point on to heaven. Aside from the fact that Purgatory is an unbiblical doctrine, the idea that sinners have another chance for salvation after death is in direct contradiction to the Bible. Scripture is clear that we are to *"seek the Lord while He may be found"* and that once we die, we are destined to judgment *(Hebrews 9:27)* based on our lives, not on anything we do after we die. There will be no "second chance" for salvation beyond this life. As long as a person is alive, he has a second, third, fourth, fifth, etc. chance to accept Christ and be saved *(John 3:16; Romans 10:9-10; Acts 16:31)*. Furthermore, the idea that a sinner can "correct" his nature, either before or after death, is contrary to biblical revelation, which says clearly that only Christ can overcome the sin nature, imparting to believers a completely new nature *(2 Corinthians 5:17)*.

In the other two parts of the Divine Comedy, Dante imagines again various levels of both hell and heaven. In the Inferno, he describes in great detail the torments and agonies of hell; these do not come from the Bible, but from his own vivid imagination. Some have speculated that perhaps these terrible images spring from Dante's doubt about his own salvation. In any case, the major differences between Inferno and the Bible's depiction of hell are these:

- Levels of hell. Dante describes nine concentric circles, representing an increase of wickedness, where sinners are punished in a fashion befitting their crimes. The Bible says nothing of varying levels of punishment in hell, nor of different levels of severity of sin. The universal punishment for all who reject Jesus Christ as Savior is to be *"cast into the lake of fire" (Revelation 20:15)*. As far as sin is concerned, the Bible declares that failing to keep God's law in even the smallest aspect makes us guilty of all of it and therefore worthy of eternal punishment *(James 2:10)*. The murderer, the liar and the proud man are all equally guilty in God's eyes and all earn the same punishment.

- Different types of punishment. Dante's vision of hell involved such eternal punishments as souls tormented by biting insects, wallowing in mire, immersed in boiling blood, being lashed with whips. Lesser punishments involve having heads on backwards, chasing unreachable goals for eternity, and walking endlessly in circles. The Bible, however, speaks of hell as a place of *"outer darkness"* where there will be *"weeping and gnashing of teeth" (Matthew 8:12, 22:13)*. Whatever punishments await the unrepentant sinner in hell are no doubt more hideous than even Dante could imagine.

- The final section of the poem, "Paradiso," is Dante's vision of heaven. Here Dante is guided through nine spheres, again in a concentric pattern, each level coming closer to the presence of God. Dante's heaven is depicted as having souls in a hierarchy of spiritual development, based at least in part on their human ability to love God. Here are nine levels of people who have attained, by their own efforts, the sphere in which they now reside, by some work of sacrifice, good deeds, or love. The Bible, however, is clear that no amount of good works can earn heaven; only faith in the shed blood of Christ on the cross and the righteousness of Christ imputed to us can save us and destine us for heaven *(Matthew 26:28; 2 Corinthians*

5:21). In addition, the idea that we have to work our way through areas of heaven to come before God is unknown in the Scriptures. Heaven will be a place of unbroken fellowship with God, where we will serve Him and *"see His face" (Revelation 22:3-4)*. All believers will forever enjoy the pleasure of God's company, made possible by our faith in His Son.

- Throughout the Divine Comedy, the theme of salvation by man's works is prevalent. Purgatory is seen as a place where sins are purged through the sinner's efforts, and heaven has differing levels of rewards for works done in life. Even in the afterlife, Dante sees man as continually working and striving for reward and relief from punishment. But the Bible tells us that heaven is a place of rest from striving, not a continuation of it. The Apostle John writes, *"Then I heard a voice from heaven say, 'Write: Blessed are the dead who die in the Lord from now on.' 'Yes,' says the Spirit, 'they will rest from their labor, for their deeds will follow them.'"* Believers who live and die in Christ are saved by faith alone, and the very faith which gets us to heaven is His *(Hebrews 12:2)*, as are the works we do in that faith *(Ephesians 2:10)*. The Divine Comedy may be of interest to Christians as a literary work, but the Bible alone is our infallible guide for faith and life and is the only source of eternal truth.

48. Question: "Is Luke 16:19-31 a parable or an account of events that actually occurred?"

Luke 16:19-31 has been the focus of much controversy. Some take the story of the rich man and Lazarus to be a true, historical account of events that actually occurred; others consider it a parable or allegory.

Those who interpret this narrative as a true incident have several reasons for doing so. First, the story is never called a parable. Many other of Jesus' stories are designated as parables, such as the sower and the seed *(Luke 8:4)*; the prosperous farmer *(Luke 12:16)*; the barren fig tree *(Luke 13:6)*; and the wedding feast *(Luke 14:7)*. Second, the story of the rich man and Lazarus uses the actual name of a person. Such specificity would set it apart from ordinary parables, in which the characters are not named.

Third, this particular story does not seem to fit the definition of a parable, which is a presentation of a spiritual truth using an earthly illustration. The story of the rich man and Lazarus presents spiritual truth directly, with no earthly metaphor. The setting for most of the story is the afterlife, as opposed to the parables, which unfold in earthly contexts.

In contrast, others maintain that this story is a parable and not an actual incident that occurred. They point out that Jesus' standard practice was to use parables in His teaching. They do not consider the above arguments strong enough to warrant classifying the story as anything but a parable. Also, there are some aspects of the account that do not seem to agree with the rest of Scripture. For example, can people in hell and people in heaven see each other and speak to each other?

The important thing is that whether the story is a true incident or a parable, the teaching behind it remains the same. Even if it is not a "real" story, it is realistic. Parable or not, Jesus plainly used this story to teach that after death the unrighteous are eternally separated from God, that they remember their rejection of the Gospel, that they are in torment, and that their condition cannot be remedied. In *Luke 16:19-31*, whether parable or literal account, Jesus clearly taught the existence of heaven and hell as well as the deceitfulness of riches to those who trust in material wealth.

49. Question: "Where is heaven? What is the location of heaven?"

Heaven is most certainly a real place. The Bible very definitely speaks of heaven's existence, and access to heaven through faith in Jesus Christ, but there are no verses that give us a Mapquest-style location. The short answer to this question is, *"heaven is where God is."* The place referred to in this question is called the *"third heaven"* and *"paradise"* in *2 Corinthians 12:1-4*, where the apostle Paul tells of a living man who was "caught up" to heaven and was unable to describe it. The Greek word translated "caught up" is also used in *1 Thessalonians 4:17* in describing the rapture, wherein believers will be caught up to be with the Lord. These passages have led to the conclusion that heaven is beyond the earth's airspace and beyond the stars.

However, since God is spirit, "heaven" cannot signify a place remote from us which He inhabits. The Greek gods were thought of as spending most of their time far away from earth in sort of a celestial equivalent of the Bahamas, but the God of the Bible is not like this. He is always near us when we call on Him *(James 4:8)*, and we are encouraged to *"draw near"* to Him *(Hebrews 10:1, 22)*. Granted, the "heaven" where saints and angels dwell has to be thought of as a sort of locality, because saints and angels, as God's creatures, exist in space and time. But when the Creator is said to be "in heaven," the thought is that He exists on a different plane from us, rather than in a different place.

That God in heaven is always near to His children on earth is something which the Bible expresses throughout. The New Testament mentions heaven with considerable frequency. Yet, even with this frequency, detailed description of its location is missing. Perhaps God has intentionally covered its location in mystery, for it is more important for us to focus on the God of heaven than the description or location of it. It is more important to know the why than the where. The New Testament focuses on the purpose of heaven more than telling us what it is like or where it is. We have seen that hell is for separation and punishment *(Matthew 8:12; 22:13)*. Heaven, on the other hand, is for fellowship and eternal joy and, more importantly, worshipping around the throne of God.

50. Question: "Where is hell? What is the location of hell?"

Various theories on the location of hell have been put forward. A traditional view is that hell is in the center of the earth. Others propose that hell is located in outer space in a black hole. In the Old Testament, the word translated "hell" is *Sheol*; in the New Testament, it's *Hades* (meaning "unseen") and *Gehenna* ("the Valley of Hinnom"). *Sheol* is also translated as "pit" and "grave." Both Sheol and Hades refer to a temporary abode of the dead before judgment (*Psalm 9:17; Revelation 1:18*). Gehenna refers to an eternal state of punishment for the wicked dead (*Mark 9:43*).

The idea that hell is below us, perhaps in the center of the earth, comes from passages such as *Luke 10:15: "And thou, Capernaum, which art exalted to heaven, shalt be thrust down to hell" (KJV)*. Also, in *1 Samuel 28:13-15*, the medium of Endor sees the spirit of Samuel *"coming up out of the ground."* We should note, however, that neither of these passages is concerned with the geographic location of hell. Capernaum's being thrust "down" is probably a reference to their being condemned rather than a physical direction. And the medium's vision of Samuel was just that: a vision.

In the King James Version, *Ephesians 4:9* says that before Jesus ascended into heaven, *"he also descended...into the lower parts of the earth."* Some Christians take *"the lower parts of the earth"* as a reference to hell, where they say Jesus spent the time between His death and resurrection. However, the New International Version gives a better translation: "he also descended to the lower, earthly regions." This verse simply says that Jesus came to earth. It's a reference to His incarnation, not to His location after death.

The notion that hell is somewhere in outer space, possibly in a black hole, is based on the knowledge that black holes are places of great heat and pressure from which nothing, not even light, can escape. Surprisingly, this concept of hell is presented in the 1979 Walt Disney film "The Black Hole". Near the movie's end, all the characters pass through a black hole. On the other side, the villain finds himself in a fiery place of torment, while the other characters enjoy disembodied bliss. It's interesting that a Disney movie would include a depiction of hell, but its best not to base our theology on movies!

Another speculation is that the earth itself will be the "lake of fire" spoken of in *Revelation 20:10-15*. When the earth is destroyed by fire (*2 Peter 3:10; Revelation 21:1*), the theory goes, God will use that burning sphere as the everlasting place of torment for the ungodly. Again, this is mere speculation.

To sum up, Scripture does not tell us the geological (or cosmological) location of hell. Hell is a literal place of real torment, but we do not know where it is. Hell may have a physical location in this universe, or it may be in an entirely different "dimension." Whatever the case, the location of hell is far less important than the need to avoid going there.

51. Question: "When will the Resurrection take place?"

The Bible is clear that resurrection is a reality and this life is not all that there is. While death is the end of physical life, it is not the end of human existence. Many erroneously believe that there is one general resurrection at the end of the age, but the Bible teaches that there will be not one resurrection, but a series of resurrections, some to eternal life in heaven and some to eternal damnation (*Daniel 12:2; John 5:28-29*).

The first great resurrection was the resurrection of Jesus Christ. It is documented in each of the four Gospels (*Matthew 28; Mark 16; Luke 24; John 20*), cited several times in *Acts* (*Acts 1:22; 2:31; 4:2, 33; 26:23*), and mentioned repeatedly in the letters to the churches (*Romans 1:4; Philippians 3:10; 1 Peter 1:3*). Much is made of the importance of Christ's resurrection in *1 Corinthians 15:12-34*, which records that over five hundred people saw Him at one of His post-resurrection appearances. Christ's resurrection is the "first fruits" or guarantee to every Christian that he will also be resurrected. Christ's resurrection is also the basis of the Christian's certainty that all people who have died will one day be raised to face fair and even-handed judgment by Jesus Christ (*Acts 17:30-31*). The resurrection to eternal life is described as *"the first resurrection" (Revelation 20:5-6)*; the resurrection to judgment and torment is described as *"the second death" (Revelation 20:6, 13-15)*.

The first great resurrection of the Church will occur at the time of the rapture. All those who have placed their trust in Jesus Christ during the Church Age, and have died before Jesus returns, will be resurrected at the rapture. The Church Age began on the Day of Pentecost and will end when Christ returns to take believers back to heaven with Him (*John 14:1-3; 1 Thessalonians 4:16-17*). The Apostle Paul explained that not all Christians will die, but all will be changed, i.e., given resurrection-type bodies (*1 Corinthians 15:50-58*), some without having to die! Christians who are alive, and those who have already died, will be caught up to meet the Lord in the air and be with Him always!

Another great resurrection will occur when Christ returns to earth (His Second Coming) at the end of the Tribulation period. After the rapture, the Tribulation is the next event after the Church Age in God's chronology. This will be a time of terrible judgment upon the world, described in great detail in *Revelation 6-18*. Though all Church Age believers will be gone, millions of people left behind on earth will come to their senses during this time and will trust in Jesus as their Savior. Tragically, most of them will pay for their faith in Jesus by losing their lives (*Revelation 6:9-11; 7:9-17; 13:7, 15-17; 17:6; 19:1-2*). These believers in Jesus who die during the Tribulation will be resurrected at Christ's return and will reign with Him for a thousand years during the Millennium (*Revelation 20:4, 6*). Old Testament believers such as Job, Noah, Abraham, David and even John the Baptist (who was assassinated before the Church began) will be resurrected at this time also. Several passages in the Old Testament mention this event *(Job 19:25-27; Isaiah 26:19; Daniel 12:1-2; Hosea 13:14). Ezekiel 37:1-14* describes primarily the re-gathering of the Nation of Israel using the symbolism of dead corpses coming back to life. But from the language used, a physical resurrection of dead Israelis cannot be excluded from the passage. Again, all believers in God (in the Old Testament era) and all believers in Jesus (in the New Testament era) participate in the first resurrection, a resurrection to life (*Revelation 20:4, 6*).

There may be another resurrection at the end of the Millennium, one which is implied, but never explicitly stated in Scripture. It is possible that some believers will die a physical death during the Millennium. Through the prophet Isaiah, God said, *"No longer will there be in it an infant who lives but a few days, or an old man who does not live out his days; for the youth will die at the age of one hundred and the one who does not reach the age of one hundred will be thought accursed" (Isaiah 65:20).* On the other hand, it is also possible that death in the Millennium will only come to the disobedient. In either event, some kind of transformation will be required to fit believers in their natural bodies in the Millennium for pristine existence throughout eternity. Each believer will need to have a "resurrected" type of body.

It is clear from Scripture that God will destroy the entire universe, including the earth, with fire (*2 Peter 3:7-12*). This will be necessary to purge God's creation of its endemic evil and decay brought upon it by man's sin. In its place God will create a new heaven and a new earth (*2 Peter 3:13; Revelation 21:1-4*). But what will happen to those believers who survived the Tribulation and entered the Millennium in their natural bodies? And what will happen to those who were born during the Millennium, trusted in Jesus, and continued to live in their natural bodies? Paul has made it clear that flesh and blood, which is mortal and able to decay, cannot inherit the kingdom of God. That eternal kingdom is inhabitable only by those with resurrected, glorified bodies that are no longer mortal and are not able to decay (*1 Corinthians 15:35-49*). Presumably, these believers will be given resurrection bodies without having to die. Precisely when this happens is not explained, but theologically, it must happen somewhere in the transition from the old earth and universe to the new earth and new heaven (*2 Peter 3:13; Revelation 21:1-4*).

There is a final resurrection, apparently of all the unbelieving dead of all ages. Jesus Christ will raise them from the dead (*John 5:25-29*) after the Millennium, the thousand-year reign of Christ (*Revelation 20:5*), and after the destruction of the present earth and universe (*2 Peter 3:7-12; Revelation 20:11*). This is the resurrection described by Daniel as an awakening *"from the dust of the ground ... to disgrace and everlasting contempt"* (*Daniel 12:2*). It is described by Jesus as a *"resurrection of judgment"* (*John 5:28-29*).

The Apostle John saw something that would happen in the future. He saw a *"great white throne"* (*Revelation 20:11*). Heaven and earth *"fled away"* from the One sitting on it. This is evidently a description of the dissolution by fire of all matter, including the entire universe and earth itself (*2 Peter 3:7-12*). All the (godless) dead will stand before the throne. This means they have been resurrected after the thousand years (*Revelation 20:5*). They will possess bodies that can feel pain but will never cease to exist (*Mark 9:43-48*). They will be judged, and their punishment will be commensurate with their works. But there is another book opened, the Lamb's book of life (*Revelation 21:27*). Those

68

whose names are not written in the book of life are cast into the *"lake of fire,"* which amounts to *"the second death"* (*Revelation 20:11-15*). No indication is given of any who appear at this judgment that their names are found in the book of life. Rather, those whose names appear in the book of life were among those who are blessed, for they received forgiveness and partook of the first resurrection, the resurrection to life (*Revelation 20:6*).

52. Question: "What is the intermediate state?"

The "intermediate state" is a theological concept that speculates regarding what kind of body, if any, believers in heaven have while they wait for their physical bodies to be resurrected. The Bible makes it clear that deceased believers are with the Lord (*2 Corinthians 5:6-8; Philippians 1:23*). The Bible also makes it clear that the resurrection of believers has not yet occurred, meaning that the bodies of deceased believers are still in the grave (*1 Corinthians 15:50-54; 1 Thessalonians 4:13-17*). So, the question of the intermediate state is whether believers in heaven are given temporary physical bodies until the resurrection, or whether believers in heaven exist in spiritual/non-corporeal form until the resurrection.

The Bible does not give a great amount of detail regarding the intermediate state. The only Scripture that specifically, but indirectly, speaks to the issue is *Revelation 6:9*, *"... I saw under the altar the souls of those who had been slain because of the word of God and the testimony they had maintained."* In this verse John is given a vision of those who will be killed because of their faith during the end times. In this vision those believers who had been killed are under God's altar in heaven and are described as "souls." So, from this one verse, if there is a biblical answer for the intermediate state, it would seem that believers in heaven are in spiritual/non-corporeal form until the resurrection.

The heaven that ultimately awaits believers is the New Heavens and New Earth (*Revelation 21-22*). Heaven will indeed be a physical place. Our physical bodies will be resurrected and glorified, made perfectly fit for eternity on the New Earth. Currently, heaven is a spiritual realm. It would seem, then, that there would be no need for temporary physical bodies if believers are in a spiritual heaven. Whatever the intermediate state is, we can rest assured that believers in heaven are perfectly content, enjoying the glories of heaven and worshipping the majesty of the Lord.

53. Question: "What is the difference between Sheol, Hades, Hell, the lake of fire, Paradise, and Abraham's bosom?"

The different terms used in the Bible for heaven and hell - sheol, hades, gehenna, the lake of fire, paradise, and Abraham's bosom - are the subject of much debate and can be confusing.

The word "paradise" is used as a synonym for heaven (*2 Corinthians 12:4; Revelation 2:7*). When Jesus was dying on the cross and one of the thieves being crucified with Him asked Him for mercy, Jesus replied, *"I tell you the truth, today you will be with me in paradise" (Luke 23:43)*. Jesus knew that His death was imminent and that He would soon be in heaven with His Father. Therefore, Jesus used paradise as a synonym for heaven, and the word has come to be associated with any place of ideal loveliness and delight.

Abraham's bosom is referred to only once in the Bible, in the story of Lazarus and the rich man (*Luke 16:19-31*). It was used in the Talmud as a synonym for heaven. The image in the story is of Lazarus reclining at a table leaning on Abraham's breast, as John leaned on Jesus' breast at the Last Supper, at the heavenly banquet. There are differences of opinion about what exactly Abraham's bosom represents. Those who believe the setting of the story is a period after the Messiah's death and resurrection see Abraham's bosom as synonymous with heaven. Those who believe the setting to be prior to the crucifixion see Abraham's bosom as another term for paradise. The setting is really irrelevant to the point of the story, which is that wicked men will see the righteous in happiness, and themselves in torment, and that a "great gulf" exists between them (*Luke 16:26*) which will never be spanned.

In the Hebrew Scriptures, the word used to describe the realm of the dead is *sheol*. It simply means the "place of the dead" or the "place of departed souls/spirits." The New Testament Greek word that is used for hell is "hades," which also refers to "the place of the dead." The Greek word *gehenna* is also used in the New Testament for hell and is derived from the Hebrew word *hinnom*. Other Scriptures in the New Testament indicate that sheol/hades is a temporary place where the souls of unbelievers are kept as they await the final resurrection and judgment at the Great White Throne judgment. The souls of the righteous go directly into the presence of God, heaven/paradise/Abraham's bosom, at death (*Luke 23:43; 2 Corinthians 5:8; Philippians 1:23*).

The lake of fire, mentioned only in *Revelation 19:20* and *20:10, 14-15*, is the final hell, the place of eternal punishment for all unrepentant rebels, both angelic and human (*Matthew 25:41*). It is described as a place of burning sulfur, and those in it experience eternal, unspeakable agony of an unrelenting nature (*Luke 16:24; Mark 9:45-46*). Those who have rejected Christ and are in the temporary abode of the dead in hades/sheol have the lake of fire as their final destination.

But those whose names are written in the Lamb's book of life should have no fear of this terrible fate. By faith in Christ and His blood shed on the cross for our sins, we are destined to live eternally in the presence of God

54. Question: "Will we be able to see all three members of the Trinity in Heaven?"

Before considering if we will actually be able to see God the Father, the Son and the Holy Spirit, we need to establish that they are three Persons. Without delving too deeply into the doctrine of the Trinity, we need to understand that the Father is not the same Person as the Son, the Son is not the same Person as the Holy Spirit and the Holy Spirit is not the same Person as the Father. They are not three Gods. They are three distinct Persons, yet they are all the one God. Each has a will, can speak, can love, etc., and these are demonstrations of personhood.

They are in absolute perfect harmony consisting of one substance. They are coeternal, coequal and co-powerful. If any one of the three were removed, there would be no God.

So in heaven, there are three Persons. But will we be able to actually see them? *Revelation 4:3-6* gives us a description of heaven and the throne that is occupied by God and by the Lamb: *"the one sitting there had the appearance of jasper and carnelian... a rainbow resembling an emerald encircled the throne. Before the throne... a sea of glass, clear as crystal."* Since God dwells in *"unapproachable light"* and is one *"whom no one has seen or can see" (1 Timothy 6:16)*, God is described in terms of the reflected brilliance of precious stones. *1 Corinthians 2:9* says, *"No eye has seen, no ear has heard, no mind has conceived what God has prepared for those who love him."* Because of God's holiness, it may be that we will never be able to look upon His face, but again, this is speculation.

Revelation 5:6 tells us that in heaven, the Lamb stands in the center of the throne and there are descriptions of Him clothed in brilliant white. Since the Lamb represents Christ Jesus, and we know that human eyes have beheld Him after His resurrection and glorification, it seems reasonable to conclude that in heaven, we will be able to look upon our Lord and Savior.

The Holy Spirit, by the very nature of His being, is able to move at will and take various forms. When Jesus was baptized, the Holy Spirit descended on Him in the form of a dove (*Matthew 3:13-17*). At Pentecost, the Holy Spirit was accompanied by a loud rushing noise and was seen as tongues of fire (*Acts 2:1-4*). It may not be possible to see the Holy Spirit unless He chooses to manifest Himself in some form, but that is speculation.

Mere mortals do not have the ability to grasp the wonders of heaven - it is entirely beyond our comprehension. Whatever heaven is like, it will far exceed our wildest imaginings! All we know is that we will be worshiping our great God and full of wonder that He died to save sinners.

55. Question: "Is hell literally a place of fire and brimstone?"

By raining down fire and brimstone upon the cities of Sodom and Gomorrah, God not only demonstrated how He felt about overt sin, but He also launched an enduring metaphor. After the events of *Genesis 19:24*, the mere mention of fire, brimstone, Sodom or Gomorrah instantly transports a reader into the context of God's judgment. Such an emotionally potent symbol, however, has trouble escaping its own gravity. This fiery image can impede, rather than advance, its purpose. A symbol should show a similarity between two *dissimilar* entities. Fire and brimstone describes some of what hell is *like*, but not all of what hell *is*.

The word the Bible uses to describe a burning hell, Gehenna, comes from an actual burning place, the valley of Gehenna adjacent to Jerusalem on the south. Gehenna is an English transliteration of the Greek form of an Aramaic word, which is derived from the Hebrew phrase "the Valley of (the son[s] of) Hinnom." In one of their greatest apostasies, the Jews (especially under kings Ahaz and Manasseh) passed their children through the fires in sacrifice to the god Molech in that very valley (*2 Kings 16:3; 2 Chronicles 33:6; Jeremiah 32:35*). Eventually, the Jews considered that location to be ritually unclean (2 Kings 23:10), and they defiled it all the more by casting the bodies of criminals into its smoldering heaps. In Jesus' time this was a place of constant fire, but more so, it was a refuse heap, the last stop for all items judged by men to be worthless. When Jesus spoke of *Gehenna* hell, He was speaking of the city dump of all eternity. Yes, fire was *part* of it, but the purposeful casting away - the separation and loss - was *all* of it.

In *Mark 9:43* Jesus used another powerful image to illustrate the seriousness of hell. *"If your hand causes you to sin, cut it off. It is better for you to enter life maimed than with two hands to go into hell, where the fire never goes out."* For most readers, this image *does* escape its own gravity, in spite of the goriness! Few believe that Jesus wants us literally to cut off our own hand. He would *rather* that we do whatever is necessary to avoid going to hell, and that is the purpose of such language? To polarize, to set up an either/or dynamic, to compare. Since the first part of the passage uses imagery, the second part does also, and therefore should not be understood as an encyclopedic description of hell.

In addition to fire, the New Testament describes hell as a bottomless pit (abyss) (*Revelation 20:3*), a lake (*Revelation 20:14*), darkness

(*Matthew 25:30*), death (*Revelation 2:11*), destruction (*2 Thessalonians 1:9*), everlasting torment (*Revelation 20:10*), a place of wailing and gnashing of teeth (*Matthew 25:30*), and a place of gradated punishment (*Matthew 11:20-24; Luke 12:47-48; Revelation 20:12-13*). The very *variety* of hell's descriptors argues against applying a literal interpretation of any particular one. For instance, hell's literal fire could emit no light, since hell would be literally dark. Its fire could not consume its literal fuel (persons!) since their torment is non-ending. Additionally, the gradation of punishments within hell also confounds literalness. Does hell's fire burn Hitler more fiercely than an honest pagan? Does he fall more rapidly in the abyss than another? Is it darker for Hitler? Does he wail and gnash more loudly or more continually than the other? The variety and symbolic nature of descriptors do not lessen hell, however, just the opposite, in fact. Their combined effect describes a hell that is *worse* than death, *darker* than darkness, and *deeper* than any abyss. Hell is a place with *more* wailing and gnashing of teeth than any single descriptor could ever portray. It's symbolic descriptors bring us to a place beyond the limits of our language, to a place far worse than we could ever imagine.

56. Question: "What does the Bible say about halos?"

A halo, also called a nimbus, is a geometric shape, usually in the form of a disk, circle, ring, or rayed structure. Traditionally, the halo represents a radiant light around or above the head of a divine or sacred person. Since halos are found nowhere in the Bible, what is their origin in Christianity?

Interestingly, the word "halo" comes from the Greek word for a threshing floor. It was on these floors that oxen moved round and round in a continuous circle on the ground, making a circular path in the shape we now associate with halos. Many ancient societies, including the Egyptians, Indians and Romans, used a circular sign to suggest supernatural forces, such as angels, at work.

In art, halos originally appeared as disks of gold sketched upon the head of a figure. This depicted a sphere of light radiating from the head of the person, suggesting that the subject was in a mystical state or sometimes just very smart. Because of its shape and color, the halo was also associated with the sun and resurrection. By the fourth century, the halo had become widely used in standard Christian art. Essentially, it was used to mark a figure as being in the kingdom of light. Most commonly, Jesus and the Virgin Mary are shown with halos, along with the angels. In fact, halos are found in art forms all over the world. Sometimes, especially in the East, crowns are used instead of halos, but the meaning is the same: holiness, innocence and spiritual power.

With it not being found in the Bible, the halo is both pagan and non-Christian in its origin. Many centuries before Christ, natives decorated their heads with a crown of feathers to represent their relationship with the sun god. The halo of feathers upon their heads symbolized the circle of light that distinguished the shining divinity or god in the sky. As a result, these people came to believe that adopting such a nimbus or halo transformed them into a kind of divine being.

However, interestingly enough, before the time of Christ, this symbol had already been used by not only the Hellenistic Greeks in 300 B.C., but also by the Buddhists as early as the first century A.D. In Hellenistic and Roman art, the sun-god, Helios, and Roman emperors often appear with a crown of rays. Because of its pagan origin, the form was avoided in early Christian art, but a simple circular nimbus was adopted by Christian emperors for their official portraits.

From the middle of the fourth century, Christ was portrayed with this imperial attribute, and depictions of His symbol, the Lamb of God, also displayed halos. In the fifth century, halos were sometimes given to angels, but it was not until the sixth century that the halo became customary for the Virgin Mary and other saints. For a period during the fifth century, living persons of eminence were depicted with a square nimbus.

Then, throughout the Middle Ages, the halo was used regularly in representations of Christ, the angels, and the saints. Often, Christ's halo is quartered by the lines of a cross or inscribed with three bands, interpreted to signify His position in the Trinity. Round halos are typically used to signify saints, meaning those people considered as spiritually gifted. A cross within a halo is most often used to represent Jesus. Triangular halos are used for representations of the Trinity. Square halos are used to depict unusually saintly living personages.

As we've stated at the outset, the halo was in use long before the Christian era. It was an invention of the Hellenists in 300 B.C. and is not found anywhere in the Scriptures. In fact, the Bible gives us no example for the bestowal of a halo upon anyone. If anything, the halo has been derived from the profane art forms of ancient secular art traditions.

57. Question: "Going to Heaven - how can I guarantee my eternal destination?"

Face it. The day that each of us will step into eternity may come sooner than we think. In preparation for that moment, we need to know this truth, not everyone is going to heaven. How can we know for sure that we are one of those who will spend eternity in heaven? Some 2,000 years ago, the apostles Peter and John were preaching the gospel of Jesus Christ to a large crowd in Jerusalem. It was then that Peter made a profound statement that resonates even in our post-modern world: "Salvation is found in no one else, for there is no other name under heaven given to men by which we must be saved" (*Acts 4:12*).

Even as it was then, in today's "all ways lead to heaven" climate, this is not a politically correct message. There are many who think they can have heaven without having Jesus. They want the good promises of glory, but they don't want to be bothered by the cross, much less the One who hung and died there for the sins of all who would believe in Him. Many don't want to accept Jesus as the only way and are determined to find another path. But Jesus Himself warns us that no other path exists and the consequences for not accepting this truth are an eternity in hell. He has told us plainly that *"whoever believes in the Son has eternal life, but whoever rejects the Son will not see life, for God's wrath remains on him" (John 3:36)*.

Some will argue that it's extremely narrow-minded of God to provide only one way to heaven. But, frankly, in light of mankind's rebellious rejection of God, it's extremely broad-minded for Him to provide us with *any* way to heaven. We deserve judgment, and instead He gives us the way of escape by sending His only begotten Son to die for our sins. Whether someone sees this as narrow or broad, it's the truth, and Christians need to maintain the clear, untarnished message that the only way to heaven is through Jesus Christ.

Many people today have believed a watered-down gospel that does away with the message of repentance of their sins. They want to believe in a loving, nonjudgmental God who requires no repentance and no change in their lifestyle. They may say things like, "I believe in Jesus Christ, but my God is not judgmental. My God would never send a person to hell." But we cannot have it both ways. If we profess to be Christians, we must recognize Christ for who He said He is the one and only way to heaven. To deny that is to deny Jesus Himself, for it was He who declared, *"I am the way and the truth and the life. No one comes to the Father except through me" (John 14:6).*

The question still remains: who will actually enter into God's kingdom? How can I guarantee my eternal destination? The answer to these questions is seen in the clearly drawn distinction between those who have eternal life and those who do not. *"He who has the Son has life; he who does not have the Son of God does not have life" (1 John 5:12).* Those who believe in Christ, who have accepted His sacrifice in payment of their sins, and who follow Him in obedience will spend eternity in heaven. Those who reject Him will not. *"Whoever believes in him is not condemned, but whoever does not believe stands condemned already because he has not believed in the name of God's one and only Son" (John 3:18).*

As awesome as heaven will be for those who choose Jesus Christ as Savior, hell will be that much more awful for those who reject Him. Our message to the lost would be delivered with more urgency if we understood what the holiness and righteousness of God will do to those who have rejected the full provision of forgiveness in His Son, Jesus Christ. One cannot read the Bible seriously without seeing it over and over again, the line is drawn. The Bible is very clear that there is one and only one way to heaven, through Jesus Christ. He has given us this warning: *"Enter through the narrow gate. For wide is the gate and broad is the road that leads to destruction, and many enter through it. But small is the gate and narrow the road that leads to life, and only a few find it" (Matthew 7:13-14).*

There is only one way to heaven and those who follow that way are guaranteed to get there. But not everyone is following that way. Are you?

58. Question: "Will we be naked in Heaven?"

Since Adam and Eve were naked in the Garden of Eden before the Fall (*Genesis 3*), and since the New Earth will be a restored paradise Earth, some speculate that in eternity, we will be naked as well. While there would be nothing wrong with glorified believers in Heaven being naked, that does not seem to be the case. Angelic beings and those who have been redeemed are always described as wearing some kind of garments. In Daniel's vision, the angel (whether it was an angelic being or a preincarnate appearance of Christ) was dressed in linen with a belt of fine gold around his waist. Similarly, the angel guarding Jesus' tomb was described as wearing garments: *"His countenance was like lightning, and his raiment white as snow" (Matthew 28:3).*

In heaven, we will not be naked as Adam and Eve were before they sinned. Their nakedness was symbolic of their innocence and sinlessness. When we get to heaven, having never been in a sinless state, we will be covered by the clothing that was provided by the sacrifice of Christ on the cross (*Revelation 3:18*). Since we will not have physical bodies such as we have here, we will not have physical clothing. Rather, our clothing will be part of our perfected nature. In *Revelation 4:4*, the 24 elders around the throne of God wear white clothing and golden crowns. *Revelation 3:5* tells us that those who belong to Christ will be dressed in white. Therefore, we will be clothed in His righteousness and perfection.

59. Question: "What happens at the final judgment?"

The first thing to understand about the final judgment is that it cannot be avoided. Regardless of how we may choose to interpret the end times, we are told that "it is appointed to men once to die, but after this the judgment" (Hebrews 9:27). Just as John graphically recorded in the last book of the Bible, each of us will one day find ourselves standing before God. No one will escape this climactic moment, his divine appointment with our Creator:

"And I saw a great white throne, and Him sitting on it, from whose face the earth and the heaven fled away. And a place was not found for them. And I saw the dead, the small and the great, stand before God. And books were opened, and another book was opened, which is the Book of Life. And the dead were judged out of those things which were written in the books, according to their works. And the sea gave up the dead in it. And death and hell delivered up the dead in them. And each one of them was judged according to their works. And death and hell were cast into the Lake of Fire. This is the second death. And if anyone was not found having been written in the Book of Life, he was cast into the Lake of Fire" (Revelation 20:11-15).

This remarkable passage introduces to us the final judgment, the end of human history and the beginning of the eternal state. We can be sure of this: no mistakes will be made in our hearings because we will be judged by a perfect God (*Matthew 5:48; 1 John 1:5*). This will manifest itself in many undeniable proofs. First, God will be perfectly just and fair (*Acts 10:34; Galatians 3:28*). Second, God cannot be deceived (*Galatians 6:7*). Third, God cannot be swayed by any prejudices, excuses or lies (*Luke 14:16-24*).

As God the Son, Jesus Christ will be the judge. All unbelievers will be judged by Christ, and they will be punished according to the works they have done. The Bible is very clear that unbelievers are storing up wrath against themselves (*Romans 2:5*) and that God will *"give to each person according to what he has done" (Romans 2:6)*. Believers will also be judged by Christ, but since Christ's righteousness has been imputed to us and our names are written in the book of life, we will be rewarded, but not punished, according to our deeds. At the final judgment our fate will be in the hands of the omniscient God who will judge us according to our soul's condition. Therefore, the final judgment will be a time of rejoicing for a few and the ultimate nightmare for everyone else. Jesus said that only a few would be saved while the rest would be lost *(Matthew 7:13-14)*.

However, for now, our fate is in our own hands. The end of our soul's journey will be either in an eternal heaven or in an eternal hell *(Matthew 25:46)*. We must choose where we will be by accepting or rejecting the sacrifice of Christ on our behalf, and we must make that choice before our physical lives on this earth come to an end. After death, there is no longer a choice, and our fate is to stand before the throne of God, where everything will be open and naked before Him *(Hebrews 4:13)*. *Romans 2:6* declares that what we do in our lives goes into the books that will be opened at our judgment. God *"will give to each person according to what he has done."* It is on that final judgment day that God will open His arms and declare those profound words, the very essence of our fervent hope upon this earth, *"Enter into the joy of your Lord" (Matthew 25:21)*.

60. Question: "What will be the purpose of the walls around the New Jerusalem?"

Beginning with *Revelation 21:9*, John records his final vision picturing the city of God, the New Jerusalem where believers in Christ will spend their eternal lives. The New Jerusalem is the ultimate fulfillment of all of God's promises. It exemplifies the total goodness of God, its infinite brilliance *"like that of a very precious jewel, like as jasper, clear as crystal" (Revelation 21:11)*. It is here that Scripture gives us a description so magnificent that we are able to get a glimpse of the glories of eternal heaven. In this passage, an angel of God has taken John to the top of a great and high mountain. From there John looks down upon this Holy City and tries to describe the indescribable. The city is like a massive, crystal-clear diamond with the glory of God shining from its center over all the new heavens and the new earth. All of eternity is bathed in its splendor.

Then in *verse 12*, John moves from describing its general appearance to its exterior design beginning with the walls. Human words are incapable of describing what John is trying to convey, which is why he continually uses similes, saying often "it is *like*" something else. But he gives us just enough to excite our hearts and stir our souls. God, through John, gets us as close to the understanding of this place as our finite minds can comprehend.

The walls of the city, described as "great and high," are an obvious symbol of exclusion of all that are unworthy to enter the city. Though innumerable believers will enjoy its glory, there is the chilling reminder that only the redeemed may enter. In the wall itself are twelve gates guarded by twelve angels and inscribed with the names of the twelve tribes of Israel. In keeping with the square shape of the city, the gates are located on each of the four sides as specified in *verse 13*. It is noteworthy, however, that not only are the twelve apostles represented but also the twelve tribes of Israel. This should settle beyond any question the matter of the inclusion of Old Testament saints. It apparently is the divine intent to represent that the New Jerusalem will have among its citizens not only believers of the present age, but also Israel and the saints of other ages, all of whom make up the Church of Jesus Christ.

But a final question remains: if those within the walls of the New Jerusalem are the saved, who then are those outside its walls? The last three verses of chapter 21 gives us the answer: *"On no day will its gates ever be shut, for there will be no night there. The glory and honor of the nations will be brought into it. Nothing impure will ever enter it, nor will anyone who does what is shameful or deceitful, but only those whose names are written in the Lamb's book of life" (Revelation 21:25-27)*. The city's gates in the wall will never be shut. It is not that outside of the New Jerusalem, unsaved people are still roaming around, but this pictures a city with open gates on a new earth where believers will dwell throughout eternity. Ancient cities shut their gates at night for security purposes. However, since there will be no night there, and since all evil will have been eradicated, these gates will stay open constantly. Revelation seems to picture a great amount of activity coming and going from the city, but all who go in and out are those redeemed by the blood of the Lamb. The unredeemed are a long way outside the city's walls, in the *"outer darkness"* of hell *(Matthew 8:12)*, consigned to the lake of fire *(Revelation 10:14-15)*, and can never come near the Holy City.

Jesus Himself, as well as John, specifies the "impure" as those who will not enter the city: *"Outside are the dogs who practice magic arts, the sexually immoral, the murderers, the idolaters, and everyone who loves and practices falsehood"* as well as the *"cowardly, the unbelieving, the vile, and all liars" (Revelation 22:15)*. By contrast, those people whose names are recorded in the Lamb's book of life are free to enter the Holy City; they possess life eternal and belong to their faithful Savior Jesus Christ. The Lamb, who bought them with His blood *(Rev. 5:9)*, will never blot out their names from His book *(Revelation 3:5)* and will grant them the right to the tree of life and entrance into the city *(Revelation 22:14)*.

Though the description of the city does not answer all our questions concerning the eternal state, the revelation given to John describes a beautiful and glorious future for all who put their trust in the living God. Conversely, it reveals to us that when the end does come, no opportunity will remain for one's repentance and acceptance into heaven. The truth is this: spiritual renewal takes place in this present life, not in the afterlife.

61. Question: "What should be the focus of a Christian funeral?"

There should be a vast difference between a Christian funeral and that of a non-believer. It is the difference between light and darkness, joy and sorrow, hope and despair, heaven and hell. A Christian funeral should, first and foremost, reflect the words of the Apostle Paul: *"Brothers, we do not want you to be ignorant about those who fall asleep, or to grieve like the rest of men, who have no hope" (1 Thessalonians 4:13)*. Paul uses the euphemism "fall asleep" to refer to those who have died in Christ. The grief of the relatives of an unsaved person is not to be compared with that of those whose loved one died knowing Jesus Christ as Lord and Savior. We grieve in a completely different way because we know we will see them again. The unsaved have no such hope, so their despair is complete and unrelenting.

Perhaps no other event in life brings us as close to the reality of eternity as death. One moment our loved one is here, breathing, communicating, heart beating, and the next moment he is gone. Even though the body remains, anyone who has been present at the moment of death knows that body is empty and the person who once inhabited it has left. If the deceased was a Christian, it is the knowledge of his destination that gives us the hope that unbelievers simply cannot experience. That hope should be the focus of a Christian funeral. The message of that hope should be clearly proclaimed, whether by formal preaching of the gospel of Christ or by memorials by those who knew the deceased and can testify that he/she lived in the light of the hope of eternal life available in Christ. If music is to be part of the funeral, it too should reflect the joy and hope being experienced at that very moment by the departed soul.

Above all, a Christian funeral should provide a glimpse into that brighter world, a world where all Christians will be reunited, where the bonds of love shall be made stronger than they were here, never again to be severed. It is only this hope that can soothe the pains of grief at parting. It is only when we can look forward to a better world, knowing we will see our loved ones again, love them again, and enjoy worshipping God with them forever that our tears are made dry. A Christian funeral should be a celebration of the joy of these glorious truths.

62. Question: "What are the heavenly crowns that believers can receive in Heaven?"

There are five heavenly crowns mentioned in the New Testament that will be awarded to believers. They are the imperishable crown, the crown of rejoicing, the crown of righteousness, the crown of glory, and the crown of life. The Greek word translated "crown" is *stephanos* (the source for the name Stephen the martyr) and means "a badge of royalty, a prize in the public games or a symbol of honor generally." Used during the ancient Greek games, it referred to a wreath or garland of leaves placed on a victor's head as a reward for winning an athletic contest. As such, this word is used figuratively in the New Testament of the rewards of heaven God promises those who are faithful. Paul's passage in *1 Corinthians 9:24-25* best defines for us how these crowns are awarded.

1. The Imperishable Crown - *(1 Corinthians 9:24-25)* *"Do you not know that those who run in a race all run, but one receives the prize? Run in such a way that you may obtain it. And everyone who competes for the prize is temperate [disciplined] in all things. Now they do it to obtain a perishable crown, but we for an imperishable crown" (NKJV)*. All things on this earth are subject to decay and will perish. Jesus urges us to not store our treasures on earth *"where moth and rust destroy, and where thieves break in and steal" (Matthew 6:19)*. This is analogous to what Paul was saying about that wreath of leaves that was soon to turn brittle and fall apart. But not so the heavenly crown; faithful endurance wins a heavenly reward which is *"an inheritance incorruptible and undefiled and that does not fade away, reserved in heaven for you" (1 Peter 1:3-5)*.

2. The Crown of Rejoicing - *(1 Thessalonians 2:19)* *"For what is our hope, or joy, or crown of rejoicing? Is it not even you in the presence of our Lord Jesus Christ at His coming?"* The apostle Paul tells us in *Philippians 4:4* to *"rejoice always in the Lord"* for all the bountiful blessings our gracious God has showered upon us. As Christians we have more in this life to rejoice about than anyone else. Luke tells us there is rejoicing even now in heaven *(Luke 15:7)*. The crown of rejoicing will be our reward where *"God will wipe away every tear...there shall be no more death, nor sorrow, nor crying. There shall be no more pain, for the former things have passed away" (Revelation 21:4)*.

3. The Crown of Righteousness - *(2 Timothy 4:8)* *"Finally, there is laid up for me the crown of righteousness, which the Lord, the righteous Judge, will give to me on that Day, and not to me only but also to all who have loved His appearing."* We inherit this crown through the righteousness of Christ which is what gives us a right to it, and without which it cannot be obtained. Because it is obtained and possessed in a righteous way, and not by force and deceit as earthly crowns sometimes are, it is an everlasting crown, promised to all who love the Lord and eagerly wait for His return. Through our enduring the discouragements, persecutions, sufferings, or even death, we know assuredly our reward is with Christ in eternity *(Philippians 3:20)*. This crown is not for those who depend upon their own sense of righteousness or of their own works. Such an attitude breeds only arrogance and pride, not a long-

ing, a fervent desire to be with the Lord.

4. The Crown of Glory - *(1 Peter 5:4) "And when the Chief Shepherd appears, you will receive the crown of glory that does not fade away."* Though Peter is addressing the elders, we must also remember that the crown will be awarded to all those who long for or love His appearing. This word "glory" is an interesting word referring to the very nature of God and His actions. It entails His great splendor and brightness. Recall Stephen who, while being stoned to death, was able to look into the heavens and see the glory of God *(Acts 7:55-56)*. This word also means that the praise and honor we bestow to God alone is due Him because of who He is *(Isaiah 42:8, 48:11; Galatians 1:5)*. It also recognizes that believers are incredibly blessed to enter into the kingdom, into the very likeness of Christ Himself. For as Paul so eloquently put it, *"For I consider that the sufferings of this present time are not worthy to be compared with the glory which shall be revealed in us" (Romans 8:18 NKJV)*.

5. The Crown of Life - *(Revelation 2:10) "Do not fear any of those things which you are about to suffer. Indeed, the devil is about to throw some of you into prison, that you may be tested, and you will have tribulation ten days. Be faithful until death, and I will give you the crown of life."* This crown is for all believers, but is especially dear to those who endure sufferings, who bravely confront persecution for Jesus, even to the point of death. In Scripture the word "life" is often used to show a relationship that is right with God. It was Jesus who said, *"I have come that they may have life and that they may have it more abundantly" (John 10:10)*. Just as things such as air, food, and water are vital for our physical lives, Jesus provides us what is required for our spiritual lives. He is the One who provides *"living water."* He is the *"bread of life" (John 4:10, 6:35)*. We know that our earthly lives will end. But we have the amazing promise that comes only to those who come to God through Jesus: *"And this is the promise that He has promised us, eternal life" (1 John 2:25)*. James tells us that this crown of life is for all those who love God *(James 1:12)*. The question then is how do we demonstrate our love for God? The apostle John answers this for us: *"For this is the love of God, that we keep His commandments. And His commandments are not burdensome" (1 John 5:3)*. As His children we must keep His commandments, obeying Him, always

remaining faithful. So, as we endure the inevitable trials, pains, heartaches, and tribulations, as long as we live, may we ever move forward, always *"looking unto Jesus, the author and finisher of our faith" (Hebrews 12:2)* and receive the crown of life that awaits us.

63. Question: "Does John 3:13 mean that no one went to Heaven before Jesus?"

John 3:13 says, "And no one has ascended up to Heaven except He who came down from Heaven, the Son of Man who is in Heaven." This verse is somewhat difficult to interpret and is often misunderstood. It is also frequently used by those who want to find contradictions in the Bible. Looking at the verse in context, *verses 10-12* especially, we see that Jesus is speaking on the subject of the authority and validity of His teaching. In *verse 13*, Jesus explains to Nicodemus why He alone is qualified to speak of these things, namely, because He is to only one who has ever gone to heaven and then come back with knowledge from heaven to teach to people.

No man, therefore, can speak of heavenly things as authoritatively as Jesus. To speak of those things requires intimate acquaintance with them and demands that they have been seen and experienced as only Jesus has. As no one has ascended into heaven and returned, so no one is qualified to speak of these things but He who came down from heaven. Jesus was saying that He alone was the one who had seen the Father, and He alone was qualified to declare God and make Him known *(John 1:18)*.

This does not mean that no one had ever gone to heaven or had been saved, for Enoch and Elijah had been borne there *(Genesis 5:24; Hebrews 11:5; 2 Kings 2:11)* and Abraham, Isaac, Jacob, and others were there. Rather, it means that no one had ascended and "returned," in such a way as to be qualified to speak of the things there. "Ascending" carries the idea of going someplace with authority. Jesus is the only one who has ever *ascended* to heaven with authority, since He is God's only Son *(John 1:14)*.

64. Question: "Do we receive mansions in heaven?"

The night before Jesus was crucified, He told His disciples that He would be leaving them and that they could not go with Him *(John 13:33)*. Peter asked where He was going and why they couldn't go with Him, and Jesus assured them that they would follow Him eventually *(John 13:36-37)*. Jesus said, *"In my Father's house are many rooms. If it were not so, would I have told you that I go to prepare a place for you? And if I go and prepare a place for you, I will come again and will take you to myself, that where I am you may be also" (John 14:2-3)*.

This saying of Jesus has confused many because of the King James Version's rendering of the words "house" and "mansions." The Greek word translated "house" means "an abode," literally or figuratively, and, by implication, "a family." The word translated "mansions" or "rooms" means literally "the act of staying or residing." So, putting the Greek together, Jesus is saying that in God's home (heaven) there will be many people in the family of God all abiding together. Within God's heavenly house, Christians will live in the presence of the Lord. This is quite different from the idea of rows of mansions on streets of gold, which is the image many people have of what Jesus was saying.

Jesus Christ prepares a place in heaven for His own, those who have come to Him in faith, and the Holy Spirit prepares the redeemed on earth for their place in heaven. *Revelation 7:9* tells us that there will be a *"great multitude in heaven that no one could number"* all standing before the throne. Here, again, the imagery is of multitudes together, not living separately in different mansions.

65. Question: "Is it wrong to want to die?"

Many people who are suffering from terminal illness, painful conditions, or intense sadness or emotional pain have wondered if we can just ask God to take our lives. Is this a form of suicide? Will God take us to heaven if we pray to die? The question that also arises is whether such a prayer is sinful.

Wanting to escape from suffering, whether emotional or physical, is a very human condition. Even the Lord Jesus Christ prayed, *"O My Father, if it be possible, let this cup pass from Me: nevertheless not as I will, but as You will" (Matthew 26:39).* This was the humanity of Jesus speaking. Jesus knew what lay ahead at the cross, but notice that He submitted to God's will. In all things, Jesus submitted Himself to the will of the Father *(John 5:30).* In the Garden, Jesus verified that there are times when it is necessary to suffer, and He willingly suffered because it was the will of the Father.

As believers we are always to pray, "Your Will be done." None of us will die before it is our time. David verifies the truth that all our days are planned out by God and nothing will shorten them outside of God's will: *"All the days ordained for me were written in your book before one of them came to be" (Psalm 139:16).* Rather than praying to die, it is better to pray for God's strength and grace to stand fast in whatever suffering we are experiencing and trust in God to determine the time and the details of our passing.

Suffering is hard, and sometimes the hardest part is the questions we have about why. Suffering is humbling, and as humans we don't like being humbled or weak and dependent. But when we ask, "Why me, Lord?" the answer may just be "Why not you?" When born again believers suffer on this earth, God has a purpose for that suffering and His plans and purposes are perfect and holy, just as He is perfect and holy. The Psalmist tells us *"As for God, His way is perfect" (Psalm 18:30).* If God's ways are perfect, then we can trust that whatever He does, and whatever He allows, is also perfect. This may not seem possible to us, but our minds are not God's mind, as He reminds us in *Isaiah 55:8-9.*

The Apostle Paul suffered from a "thorn in his flesh", an affliction that is not explained in the Bible, and three times he prayed for the Lord to remove that thorn. But God, who could have eased Paul's suffering in an instant, chose not to do so. He reminded Paul that the "thorn" was to keep him from becoming proud and "exalted above measure through the abundance of the revelations" he had been given, to keep him from exalting himself. But God did not leave Paul powerless to suffer alone. God assured him that the grace he had been given by God was "sufficient" and that God would be glorified by Paul relying on His power to sustain him. Paul's response to these truths was to be glad of his frailty and sufferings because in them God is glorified when the miracle of His power and strength are on display *(2 Corinthians 12:7-10)*. Therefore, rather than seeking to escape from suffering of any kind through death, we depend upon God and rest in Him, for His purpose in suffering will always bring glory to Him and abound to our blessing.

When we are under the intense pressure of suffering, we sometimes feel like we simply can't go on any longer. But God reminds us that there is no suffering or trial that comes upon a believer that someone else hasn't gone through before us. Other believers have suffered pain that could not be alleviated by modern medicine. Other believers have suffered persecution and hideous deaths at the hands of God-haters. Other believers have been lonely and abandoned, some imprisoned for their testimony. So we are certainly not alone. But God is always faithful, and He will not allow us to suffer or be tested above what we can withstand and will also make a way to escape so that we are able to bear up under it *(1 Corinthians 10:13)*.

Finally, to answer the question of whether it is actually sinful to pray to die, quite simply it may come down the principle *"Whatever is not of faith, is sin" (Romans 14:23)*. In other words, if our inner man says that it is sin, then to us it is sin. There is also the Scripture that says, *"Anyone, then, who knows the good he ought to do and doesn't do it, sins" (James 4:17)*. There is only one sin that keeps us out of heaven and that is the sin of rejecting the Lord Jesus Christ as our savior by being born again and receiving the gift of eternal life. But praying to God to allow us to die can be sin because doing so indicates a lack of faith. A better prayer would be "God, you have promised to sustain me through any trial. I beg you to ease my suffering or provide a way of escape through it. But in all things, not my will but yours be done. Amen."

66. Question: "Will more people go to heaven or to hell?"

The question of whether there are more people in heaven or hell is answered by Jesus Himself in one succinct passage: *"Enter by the narrow gate. For the gate is wide and the way is easy that leads to destruction, and those who enter by it are many. For the gate is narrow and the way is hard that leads to life, and those who find it are few" (Matthew 7:13-14).*

This passage tells us that only those who receive Jesus Christ and who believe in Him are given the right to become children of God *(John 1:12)*. As such, the gift of eternal life comes only through Jesus Christ to all those who believe. He said *"I am the way, and the truth, and the life. No one comes to the Father except through me" (John 14:6)*. It's not through Islam, Buddha, or other false gods of man's making. It's not for those wanting a cheap and easy way to heaven while continuing to live their own selfish and worldly lives on earth. Jesus only saves those who fully trust in Him as Savior *(Acts 4:12)*.

So, what are these two gates in *Matthew 7:13-14*? They are the entrance to two different "ways." The wide gate leads to the broad way, or road. The small narrow gate leads to the way that is narrow. The narrow way is the way of the godly, and the broad way is the way of the ungodly. The broad way is the easy way. It is attractive and self-indulgent. It is permissive. It's the inclusive way of the world, with few rules, few restrictions, and fewer requirements. Tolerance of sin is the norm where God's Word is not studied and His standards not followed. This way requires no spiritual maturity, no moral character, no commitment, and no sacrifice. It is the easy way of salvation following *"the course of this world, following the prince of the power of the air, of the spirit that is now at work in the sons of disobedience" (Ephesians 2:2)*. It is that broad way that *"seems right to a man, but end is the way to death" (Proverbs 14:12)*.

Those who preach a gospel of inclusiveness where *"all ways lead to heaven"* preach an utterly different gospel than the one Jesus preached. The gate of self-centeredness, self-absorption, and a proud, holier-than-thou mindset is the wide gate of the world that leads to hell, not the narrow gate which leads to eternal life. As a result, most people spend their lives following the masses who are on the broad road, doing what everyone else does and believing what everyone else believes.

The narrow way is the hard way, the demanding way. It is the way of recognizing that you cannot save yourself and must depend on Jesus Christ alone to save you. It's the way of self-denial and the cross. The fact that few find God's way implies that it is to be sought diligently. *"You will seek me and find me, when you seek me with all your heart" (Jeremiah 29:13).* The point is this that no one will stumble into the kingdom or wander through the narrow gate by accident. Someone asked Jesus: *"Lord, will those who are saved be few?"* He replied, *"Strive to enter through the narrow door. For many, I tell you, will seek to enter and will not be able" (Luke 13:23-24).*

Many will seek to enter that narrow door, the door of salvation, but "will not be able." They are unwilling to trust/rely on Jesus alone. They are unwilling to pay the price. It costs too much for them to give up the world. God's gate is a gate through which one cannot carry the baggage of sin and self-will, nor can one carry the accoutrements of materialism. The way of Christ is the way of the cross, and the way of the cross is the way of self-denial. Jesus said, *"If anyone would come after me, let him deny himself and take up his cross daily and follow me. For whoever would save his life will lose it, but whoever loses his life for my sake will save it" (Luke 9:23-24).*

Jesus knows that many will choose the wide gate and the broad way which leads to destruction and hell. Correspondingly, He said that only a few will choose the narrow gate. According to *Matthew 7:13-14,* there is no doubt that more will go to hell than to heaven. The question for you is, then, on which road are you?

67. Question: "What are the gates of hell?"

The phrase the "gates of hell" is translated in some versions as the "gates of Hades." The gates of hell or gates of Hades is found only once in the entire Scriptures, in *Matthew 16:18.* In this passage, Jesus is referring to the building of His church: *"And I tell you, you are Peter, and on this rock I will build my church, and the gates of hell shall not prevail against it" (Matthew 16:18).*

At this time Jesus had not yet established His church. In fact, this is the first instance of the word "church" in the New Testament. The church spoken of by Jesus is derived from the Greek *ekklasia* which means the "called out" or assembly. In other words, the church that Jesus is referencing as His church means the assembly of people who have been called out of the world by the gospel of Christ.

Bible scholars debate the actual meaning of the phrase "and the gates of hell shall not prevail against it." One of the better interpretations to the meaning of this phrase is as follows. In ancient times, the cities were surrounded by walls with gates, and in battles the gates of these cities would usually be the first place their enemies assaulted. This was because the protection of the city was determined by the strength or power of its gates.

As such, the "gates of hell" or "gates of Hades" means the power of Hades. The name "Hades" was originally the name of the god who presided over the realm of the dead and was oftentimes referred to as the "house of Hades." It designated the place to which everyone who departs this life descends, regardless of their moral character. In the New Testament, Hades is the realm of the dead, and in this verse Hades or hell is represented as a mighty city with its gates representing its power.

Jesus refers here to His impending death. Though He would be crucified and buried, He would rise from the dead and build His church. As such, Jesus is emphasizing the fact that the powers of death could not hold Him in. Not only would the church be established in spite of the powers of Hades or hell, but the church would thrive in spite of these powers. The church will never fail, though generation after generation succumbs to the power of physical death, yet other generations will arise to perpetuate the church. And it will continue until it has filled its mission on earth as Jesus has commanded:

> *"All authority in heaven and on earth has been given to me. Go therefore and make disciples of all nations, baptizing them in the name of the Father and of the Son and of the Holy Spirit, teaching them to observe all that I have commanded you. And behold, I am with you always, to the end of the age" (Matthew 28:18-20).*

It is clear that Jesus was declaring that death has no power to hold God's people captive. Its gates are not strong enough to overpower and keep imprisoned the church of God. The Lord has conquered death *(Romans 8:2; Acts 2:24)*. And because *"death no longer is master over Him" (Romans 6:9)*, it is no longer master over those who belong to Him.

Satan has the power of death and he will always use that power to try to destroy the church of Christ. But we have this promise from Jesus that His church, the "called out" will prevail: *"Yet a little while and the world will see me no more, but you will see me. Because I live, you also will live" (John 14:19)*.

68. Question: "What is the river of life?"

The precise phrase "river of life" does not appear in the Bible. However, *Revelation 22:1-2* does refer to *"the river of the water of life, as clear as crystal, flowing from the throne of God and of the Lamb."* The Apostle John, in his vision of the New Jerusalem, describes the river as flowing *"down the middle of the great street of the city."*

The "water of life" referred to here cannot be physical water as we know it because *Revelation 21:1* tells us there is *"no longer any sea."* He goes on to say that there is no need for sun or moon because the glory of God and the Lamb give it light *(Revelation 21:23)*. This would indicate that the hydrological cycle as we know it on earth does not exist in the New Jerusalem. Therefore, the water flowing from the throne is literally the water of eternal life, crystal clear to reflect the glory of God in a dazzling, never-ending stream. The fact that the stream emanates from the throne tells us that eternal life flows from God to His people.

Water is a common symbolic representation of eternal life in Scripture. Isaiah refers to drawing water from the *"wells of salvation"* with joy *(Isaiah 12:3)*. The Old Testament prophet Jeremiah rebuked the Israelites for abandoning God *"the spring of living water"* and digging for themselves their own cisterns which could not hold water *(Jeremiah 2:13)*. The Israelites had forsaken the living God, who alone provides eternal life, to chase after false idols, worldliness, and works-based religions. Men do the same today, refusing the water of life only Christ provides for a parched and dusty life of materialism and self-indulgence.

Jesus encouraged the Samaritan woman at the well to take from Him the water of (eternal) life so that she would never thirst again spiritually *(John 4:13-14)*. Those who believe in Him, He goes on to say in *John 7:38,* will have streams of living water flowing from them. Water is an appropriate and easily understood symbol for life. Just as physical water is necessary to sustain physical life on earth, living water from the Savior is necessary to sustain eternal life with Him. Jesus is both the Bread of Life *(John 6:35)* and the source of living water, sustaining His people forever.

69. Question: "Will there literally be streets of gold in heaven?"

Heaven's streets of gold are often referenced in song and poetry, but harder to find in the Bible. In fact, there is only one passage of Scripture that references streets of gold and that is in the Holy City, the new Jerusalem: *"...the great street of the city was of gold, as pure as transparent glass" (Revelation 21:1, 21)*. So does this verse tell us that there will literally be streets of gold in heaven? And if so, what is the importance or significance of literal streets of gold?

The Greek word translated "gold" is *chrusion* which can mean "gold, gold jewelry, or overlay." So to translate it "gold" makes complete and perfect sense. In fact, struggles of interpretation often come up when people attempt to determine which parts of the Bible to take literally and which parts to take figuratively. A good rule of thumb when studying the Bible is to take everything literally, unless it doesn't make sense to do so. And in this chapter of *Revelation*, John isn't just throwing out random descriptive terms. In the early parts of *Revelation 21*, he is given a rod to measure out the city *(v.15)*, and he specifically describes the wall of heaven as being composed of Jasper and the city itself also of gold *(v.18)*. He also describes the foundations of the city walls being comprised of many specific precious stones and jewels *(v.19-20)*. So with these specifics in mind, the description of golden streets makes perfect sense in comparison to the rest of John's eyewitness description.

So if heaven's streets are made of gold, what is the point? First, notice the condition of the gold. When gold is uncovered on earth, it is not in the desirable condition that jewelers are looking for. The gold must be smelted in order that impurities float to the top for removal, leaving only the pure gold behind. The gold that John saw in heaven was of such quality that it appears to be transparent in order to reflect the pure light of God's blazing glory. And God's ability to purify is not confined only to gold; God has purified all who will enter His heaven through the blood of Jesus Christ. *"If we confess our sins, He is faithful and just to forgive us our sins and purify us from all unrighteousness"* *(1 John 1:9)*. Not only is God's holy city one of purity by His design, so are the citizens of that city.

As we investigate this idea of golden streets further, there are some teachers and scholars who do not hold to the idea that heaven's golden streets are literal. However, by looking simply at the text God has given us within the context of the entirety of John's revelation, there seems to be no reason to doubt it. However, our attention in eternity will hardly be focused on earthly treasures. While man pursues treasures like gold on earth, one day it will simply be no more than a source of pavement for the believer in heaven. No matter how many precious jewels or materials make up the physical construction of heaven, nothing will ever be of greater value than the God who loves us and died to save us.

70. Question: "Do the souls of aborted babies go to heaven?"

Abortion as we know it today was not practiced in biblical times, and the Bible never specifically mentions the issue of abortion. It is clear from the Scriptures that an unborn baby is known by the Lord, even from the time of conception *(Psalm 139:13-16)*. Although the Bible does not mention abortion or aborted babies, we do have two keys to help us unlock the answer to the question of whether the souls of aborted babies go to heaven.

The first key is from the only passage in the Bible where something specific is said about the death of infants. In *2 Samuel 12* we learn of David's affair with Bathsheba, another man's wife. David was informed by the prophet Nathan that the child produced by that union would die. David then began to fast and pray, asking the Lord to not carry out His judgment. When the child did die, David got up from praying and fasting and ate something.

When asked about this behavior, David uttered the words recorded in *2 Samuel 12:23*, *"now he is dead; why should I fast? Can I bring him back again? I shall go to him, but he shall not return to me."* David's words reflect a clear understanding that the child could not come back to earth, but David would be with his child one day in heaven. This indicates not only David's assurance of his own future in heaven *(Psalm 23:6)*, but also the assurance that his child would share that future. From this incident, we can conclude that infants, both born and unborn, are destined for heaven.

The second key to dealing with this issue is an understanding of the character or attributes of God. A study of the attributes of God helps us understand how He works. A God of pure justice would not punish children for sins they never committed, for the Bible teaches us that *"the wages of sin is death" (Romans 6:23)*. Neither an unborn child nor an aborted baby has had the opportunity to sin and therefore is not subject to the judgment reserved for sinners. Further, God reveals Himself as a God who is good *(Psalm 52:1)* and as the perfect Judge *(Genesis 18:25)*. In this Genesis passage we find Abraham express the heartfelt thought, *"Shall not the Judge of all the earth do right?"* The answer is an emphatic "yes." A good, righteous and holy God would not punish an unborn child with an eternity in hell. *Psalm 145:17* tells us, *"The LORD is righteous in all His ways, Gracious in all His works."*

Without a specific passage that answers the initial question asked about the souls of aborted babies, and based on God's love, His goodness, His righteousness, and His perfect justice, it is appropriate to conclude that these precious children are immediately in the presence of God when their lives are cut short by the act of an abortion.

71. Question: "Will we eat food in heaven?"

Many people ask whether we will eat food in heaven because eating is not only necessary to stay alive, but it is also so very enjoyable! Because eating is enjoyable, many people conclude that what is enjoyable on earth (sex, family relationships, etc.) will naturally be present in heaven. Although the Bible does not give us a detailed answer to the question of eating food in heaven, a few observations from the Scriptures are in order. It is interesting to note that when the Lord Jesus celebrated the Passover with His disciples shortly before His crucifixion, He referred to eating and drinking in the kingdom. *"Assuredly, I say to you, I will no longer drink of the fruit of the vine until that day when I drink it new in the Kingdom of God' "* (Mark 14:25). The earthly millennial kingdom is certainly in view here, and in that kingdom all who are His followers will have already received their resurrection bodies. It would appear from this statement that we, in our glorified bodies, will eat and drink in the millennial kingdom. But what about the heavenly kingdom?

When John the Apostle was given a vision of the New Jerusalem he was shown *"a pure river of water of life, clear as crystal, proceeding from the throne of God and of the Lamb. In the middle of its street, and on either side of the river, was the tree of life, which bore twelve fruits, each tree yielding its fruit every month. The leaves of the tree were for the healing of the nations. And there shall be no more curse..."* (Revelation 22:1-3). The text does not say whether we will actually eat the fruit of the tree of life, but that is certainly possible.

If we will be eating in heaven, we don't know for sure what the heavenly menu may contain, although it has been suggested that perhaps our diet will be like that of Adam and Eve in paradise before the fall. *"And God said, 'See, I have given you every herb that yields seed which is on the face of all the earth, and every tree whose fruit yields seed; to you it shall be for food'"* (Genesis 1:29).

In the end, we don't really know if, or what, we will eat in heaven. Believers only *"know in part"* (1 Corinthians 13:9). The joys of being forever with our Savior who is the Bread of Life are beyond our limited abilities to comprehend for *"...it has not yet been revealed what we shall be, but we know that when He is revealed, we shall be like Him, for we shall see Him as He is. And everyone who has this hope in Him purifies himself, even as He is pure"* (1 John 3:2-3).

72. Question: "How can it be said that we have everlasting life when we still die?"

The Word of God assures us that all who believe in the Lord Jesus Christ will have everlasting life *(John 3:16, 6:47; 1 John 5:13)*. The Greek word translated "everlasting" means perpetual, eternal, forever. Perhaps the word "perpetual" best explains the biblical concept of everlasting life; it is life that, once begun, continues perpetually into eternity. This speaks to the idea that man's life is not merely physical. Rather, the true life of human beings is spiritual, and while the physical life ends, the spiritual continues throughout eternity. It is perpetual.

When God created Adam and Eve He put them in the Garden with the tree of life, intending that they would live joyously forever, both physically and spiritually, but they sinned and brought physical and spiritual death to themselves and to all subsequent generations *(Romans 5:12-14)*. God then sent Adam and Eve from the Garden and stationed cherubim to guard the way to the tree of life, and He did so because in His mercy He did not want man to live forever under the weight of sin. But sin must be punished and the only acceptable punishment to a holy God is everlasting punishment *(Mark 9:43-44)*. However, our merciful God sent His Son as a perfect sacrifice to suffer, once for all time, the punishment due mankind for sin, thereby providing a perfect way to the tree of life for anyone and everyone who believes in the Him *(1 John 5:12; Revelation 22:14)*.

We receive everlasting life by dying to our own efforts and receiving Christ Jesus into our hearts as our Lord and Savior, and when we do we are instantly reborn and made alive in Christ. We may not feel any immediate change, but there has in fact been a rebirth in the heart *(John 3:6-7)* and we are now free of the fear of death; we have the promise of God that we will never die spiritually, but instead will live forever with our Lord Jesus *(1 Thessalonians 5:9-10)*. Later, when we die physically, our soul will immediately be with the Lord, and still later when He returns, He will resurrect our bodies to meet Him in the air. As for those Christians that are alive at His return, their bodies will be resurrected *"in the twinkle of an eye"* and they will not experience even physical death *(1 Corinthians 15:51-52)*.

Jesus Christ instructed the Apostle John to write the last book of the Bible, and therein we again read about the tree of life: *"To him who overcomes, I will grant to eat of the tree of life which is in the Paradise of God'" (Revelation 2:7b).* The tree of life is, and always has been, symbolic of Jesus Christ. It is in Christ that all Christians trust, and it is in God's power that we rest, assured of our everlasting life *(1 Peter 1:3 -5).* From the moment we are reborn, God is in control of our destiny, and the one true God who created all things, including life and death and rebirth, will keep His word. Our God is all powerful and full of grace and truth *(John 1:14),* and He wants us to know that our eternal state is assured: Jesus said, *"I am the resurrection and the life; he who believes in Me will live even if he dies" (John 11:25).*

73. Question: "How is physical death related to spiritual death?"

The Bible has a great deal to say about death and, more importantly, what happens after death. Physical death and spiritual death are both a separation of one thing from another. Physical death is the separation of the soul from the body, and spiritual death is the separation of the soul from God. When understood in that way, the two concepts are very closely related, and both physical death and spiritual death are reflected in the very first references to death.

In the creation account *(Genesis 1–2),* we read how God created a variety of living beings. These animals had life, an inward element that gave movement and energy to their physical bodies. Scientists are still at a loss to explain what truly causes life, but the Bible is clear that God gives life to all things *(Genesis 1:11-28; 1 Timothy 6:13).* The life that God gave to mankind was different from that which He gave to animals. In *Genesis 2:7,* we are told that God *"breathed into his nostrils the breath of life, and man became a living soul."* Whereas animals have a purely physical life, humans have both a physical and a spiritual element of life, and the death we experience likewise has both a physical and a spiritual element.

According to *Genesis 2:17,* God told Adam that if he ate of the tree of the knowledge of good and evil, he would *"surely die."* Some skeptics have tried to use this verse to show an inconsistency in the Bible, because Adam and Eve did not die the very day they ate of that fruit. In the Hebrew, it literally says, "dying you will die." It indicates a process that has a definite starting point, and continues into the future. When they sinned *(Genesis 3:7)*, Adam and Eve immediately knew their guilt. With that guilt came shame, which caused them to try and hide from God, because they had become spiritually dead, or separated from Him.

In addition to the immediate spiritual death they experienced, they also began the process of physical death, even though it took many years for death to have its full effect. This can be better understood with the example of a flower. When you see a flower growing in a garden, you know it is alive, because it is connected to the stem and the roots, and is receiving nourishment from the ground. When you separate the flower from its life source, it still has the appearance of life, and can maintain that appearance for several days, depending on the conditions. Regardless of the care it is given, though, it is already dying, and that process cannot be reversed. The same is true for mankind.

The physical death that entered into the world with Adam's sin *(Romans 5:12)* affected all living things. It is difficult for us to conceive of a world without death, but that is what Scripture teaches was the condition before the Fall. All living things began the process of dying when sin entered the world. When physical death occurs, there is a definite separation of the life force from the body. When that separation occurs, there is nothing man can do to reverse it (even the medical community acknowledges the difference between a "clinical death" and a "biological death"). The wages of sin is death *(Romans 6:23)*, and death comes upon all men because all have sinned. Everyone is subject to physical death because of the presence of sin in this world, as well as their own personal sins. From a human perspective, physical death seems to be the ultimate punishment, but the Bible teaches there are deeper meanings of death to be considered.

The life that God breathed into Adam *(Genesis 2:7)* was more than just animal life; it was the breath of God, resulting in a being with a soul. Adam was created spiritually alive, connected to God in a special way. He enjoyed a relationship with God, but when he sinned, that relationship was broken. Spiritual death has implications both before and after physical death. Though Adam was still physically alive (but beginning the dying process), he became spiritually dead, separated from relationship with God. In this present life on earth, the effect of spiritual death is the loss of God's favor as well as the knowledge of and desire for God. Scripture is clear that everyone begins life *"dead in trespasses and sins" (Ephesians 2:1-5)*, resulting in a life focused on our sinful desires. Jesus taught that the remedy for spiritual death is a spiritual rebirth *(John 3:3-5)* through faith in Him. This rebirth is a reconnection to the source of life, which Jesus pictured in *John 15:1-6.* He is the vine, and we are the branches. Without being connected to Him, we have no life in us, but when we have Jesus, we have real life *(1 John 5:11-12).*

For those who refuse to accept God's salvation, physical death and spiritual death culminate in the "second death" *(Revelation 20:14).* This eternal death is not annihilation, as some have taught, but is a conscious, eternal punishment for sins in the lake of fire, described as being separated from the presence of the Lord *(2 Thessalonians 1:9).* Jesus also spoke of this eternal separation from God in *Matthew 25:41* and identified the conscious torment of individuals in the story of rich man and Lazarus *(Luke 16:19-31).* God is not willing that any should perish, but that all should come to repentance *(2 Peter 3:9),* so they do not have to remain spiritually dead. To repent means to turn away from sin, and includes confessing sin to God with sorrow for violating His holiness. Those who have received God's salvation have turned from death to life *(1 John 3:14),* and the second death has no power over them *(Revelation 20:6).*

74. Question: "What does it mean to be absent from the body?"

The phrase *"absent from the body"* is found in *2 Corinthians 5:6-8.* Paul states that he is confident in his eternal destiny and longs for the day when he can be "absent from the body" and be present with the Lord he loves and serves. To be "absent" from one's body simply means to die because at death, the spirit is separated from the body and moves into its eternal abode, either heaven with the Lord or hell, separated from God for eternity.

In the same way, Christians are always confident, knowing that while we are at home in the body we are absent from the presence of God.

For we walk by faith, not by sight. We are confident, yes, well pleased rather to be absent from the body and to be present with the Lord. When a born again believer dies, his soul goes immediately into the presence of the Lord. There, the soul consciously awaits the resurrection of the body. To the church at Philippi Paul wrote from a Roman prison: *"For to me, to live is Christ, and to die is gain. But if I live on in the flesh, this will mean fruit from my labor; yet what I shall choose I cannot tell. For I am hard-pressed between the two, having a desire to depart and be with Christ, which is far better. Nevertheless to remain in the flesh is more needful for you"* (Philippians 1:21-24).

Paul's desire in life was to glorify the Lord Jesus Christ. If he lived he could continue to labor for the Lord. If he faced execution, he would depart this life and be with Christ. He desired to be with his Savior, but if he remained on earth he could continue to minister to others.

There are some who believe in soul sleep, meaning that when a person dies, his body and soul sleep in the grave, awaiting the resurrection. But if this is true, why would Paul not want to live to minister as long as possible, rather than sleep in a grave? And secondly, if that were true the body and soul are never separated, it would be impossible to ever be absent from the body and present with the Lord.

We conclude, then, that believers who die are indeed absent from their physical bodies and present with the Lord in conscious bliss waiting that grand resurrection day!

75. Question: "What is Abraham's bosom?"

The term "Abraham's bosom" is found only once in the New Testament, in the story of the rich man and Lazarus *(Luke 16:19-31)*, in which Jesus was teaching about was the reality of heaven and hell. "Abraham's bosom" in this story is also translated "Abraham's side" (NIV, ESV), "next to Abraham" (CEV), "with Abraham" (NLT), and "the arms of Abraham" (NCV). These various translations speak to the enigmatic nature of the Greek word *kolpos.*

All these translations are attempting to convey the sense that Lazarus went to a place of rest, contentment, and peace, almost as though Abraham (a highly revered person in Jewish history) was the protector or patron. In a sad contrast, the rich man finds himself in torment with no one to help, assist or console him.

Contrary to some contemporary thought, the Bible does teach that both heaven and hell are real places. Each and every person who lives will spend eternity in one of these two places. These two destinies are portrayed in Jesus' story. While the rich man had lived for the day and only focused on life here on earth, Lazarus endured many hardships while trusting in God. So, verses 22 and 23 are very significant: *"So it was that the beggar died, and was carried by the angels to Abraham's bosom. The rich man also died and was buried. And being in torments in Hades, he lifted up his eyes and saw Abraham afar off, and Lazarus in his bosom."*

The word "death" literally means "separation." Physical death is the separation of our body from our soul/spirit, while spiritual death is the separation of our soul from God. Jesus taught that we ought not to fear physical death, but we should be most concerned about spiritual death. As we read in *Luke 12:4-5*, Jesus also said, *"And I say to you, My friends, do not be afraid of those who kill the body, and after that have no more that they can do. But I will show you whom you should fear: Fear Him who, after He has killed, has power to cast into hell; yes, I say to you, fear Him!"* Jesus' use of the term "Abraham's bosom" was a part of His teaching to focus the minds of His hearers on the fact that our choices to seek God or disregard Him here on earth literally affect where we spend eternity.

76. Question: "Who are the dead in Christ in 1 Thessalonians 4:16?"

Before identifying the "dead in Christ," we should note the context in which this phrase is found. The immediate context is *1 Thessalonians*

4:13-18, which deals with the question of what will happen at the return of the Lord Jesus. Paul's readers were concerned that when Christ returns, those who have died prior to then would somehow miss out. The primary purpose of this passage is to comfort those believers who have lost believing loved ones.

The message of this passage is a message of hope. Christians have hope that unbelievers do not have when they lose loved ones. There is hope beyond the grave for Christians, and part of that hope is at the return of Christ, those who have already died "will rise first." After that, Christians who are still alive will be transformed. Both groups will be "caught up" and will meet the Lord in the air. Paul closes this section with an admonition to encourage others with this hope.

In this passage, Paul uses the common euphemism of sleep to refer to those who have died in Christ, i.e., believers. Paul wants to comfort his readers that those Christians who have died prior to the return of Christ will not miss out on anything. That is why he opens this section by saying, *"But we do not want you to be uninformed, brothers, about those who are asleep, that you may not grieve as others do who have no hope" (v. 13)*.

So to answer the question, the dead in Christ are those believers who have died prior to the second coming of Christ. (Note: whether *1 Thessalonians 4* is referring to the second coming or the rapture is a matter of debate). Believers, whether dead or alive, belong to Christ. We get similar language from the Apostle in his first letter to the Corinthians when he writes, *"But each in his own order: Christ the first fruits, then at his coming those who belong to Christ" (1 Corinthians 15:23)*. The dead in Christ applies not only to Paul's original audience, but to all believers who have died in what can be termed the "inter-advental" period, or the time between the first and second comings of Christ.

Another question that may come up in this context is what happens to believers when they die? Certainly Paul uses sleep to refer to their state, but does this mean that believers experience (for lack of a better word) an unconscious sleep-like state until the future resurrection? Those who advocate this position, called soul sleep, base it on passages such as *1 Thessalonians 4:13-18*. But it should be noted that "sleep" as used here is euphemistic. It is not meant to convey actual sleep. In fact, the experience of the believer after death and before the end of the age when Christ returns is conscious, blissful communion with the Lord.

Paul hints at this in verses such as *2 Corinthians 5:6-8* and *Philippians 1:23*.

At death, the body lies in repose in the grave awaiting the resurrection of the last day, but the soul goes to be at home with the Lord. This is the doctrine of the intermediate state. Believers experience in a provisional sense the rewards that await them in heaven, while unbelievers experience a taste of their eternal torment in hell *(Luke 16:19-31)*.

77. Question: "How to get to heaven - what are the ideas from the different religions?"

There appears to be five major categories regarding how to get to heaven in the world's religions. Most believe that hard work and wisdom will lead to ultimate fulfillment, whether that is unity with god (Hinduism, Buddhism, and Baha'i) or freedom and independence (Scientology, Jainism). Others, like Unitarianism and Wicca, teach the afterlife is whatever you want it to be, and salvation is a non-issue because the sin nature doesn't exist. A few believe either the afterlife doesn't exist, or it's too unknowable to consider.

- Derivatives of the worship of the Christian-Judeo God generally hold that faith in God and/or Jesus and the accomplishment of various deeds, including baptism or door-to-door evangelism, will ensure the worshiper will go to heaven. Only Christianity teaches that salvation is a free gift of God through faith in Christ *(Ephesians 2:8-9)*, and no amount of work or effort is necessary or possible to get to heaven.
- Atheism: Some atheists believe there is no heaven, no afterlife at all. Upon death, people simply cease to exist. Others attempt to define the afterlife using quantum mechanics and other scientific methods.
- Baha'i: Like many other religions, Baha'i doesn't teach that man was born with a sin nature or that man needs saving from evil. Man simply needs saving from his erroneous beliefs of

how the world works and how he is to interact with the world. God sent messengers to explain to people how to come to this knowledge: Abraham, Krishna, Zoroaster, Moses, Buddha, Jesus, Muhammad, and Baha'u'llah. These prophets progressively revealed the nature of God to the world. Upon death, a person's soul continues its spiritual journey, perhaps through the states known as heaven and hell, until it comes to a final resting point, united with god.

- Buddhism: Buddhism also believes that heaven, or "Nirvana," is to be rejoined in spirit with god. Reaching Nirvana, a transcendental, blissful, spiritual state, requires following the Eightfold Path. This includes understanding the universe, and acting, speaking, and living in the right manner and with the right intentions. Mastering these and the other eight paths will return a worshipper's spirit to god.

- Chinese Religion: Chinese Religion is not an organized church, but an amalgamation of different religions and beliefs including Taoism and Buddhism. Upon death, worshipers are judged. The good are sent either to a Buddhist paradise or a Tao dwelling place. The bad are sent to hell for a period of time and then reincarnated.

- Christianity: Christianity is the only religion that teaches man can do nothing to earn or pay his way into heaven. Man, a slave to the sin nature he was born with, must completely rely on the grace of God in applying Jesus Christ's sacrifice to the sins of the believer. Upon death, the spirits of Christians go to a temporary paradise, while the spirits of unbelievers go to another temporary holding place. At the final judgment, Christians are given a new body and spend eternity with God in paradise, while unbelievers are separated from God for eternity in hell.

- Confucianism: Confucianism concentrates on appropriate behavior in life, not a future heaven. The afterlife is unknowable, so all effort should be made to make this life the best it can be, to honor ancestors, and to respect elders.

- Eastern Orthodox: Orthodoxy is a Christian-Judeo derivative that reinterprets key Scripture verses in such a way that works become essential to reach heaven. They believe faith in Jesus is necessary for salvation, but where Christianity teaches that becoming more Christ-like is the result of Christ's influence in a believer's life. Orthodoxy teaches that it is a part of the salvation process. As a result, they believe if that process (called *theosis*) is not performed appropriately, a worshiper can lose his/her salvation. After death, the devout live in an intermediate state where this *theosis* can be completed. Those who have belief but did not accomplish sufficient progress in *theosis* are sent to a temporary "direful condition" and will go to hell unless the living devout pray and complete acts of mercy on their behalf. After final judgment, the devout are sent to heaven and the others to hell. Heaven and hell are not locations, but reactions to being in the presence of God, as there is nowhere that He is not present. For Christ-followers, God's presence is paradise, but for the unsaved, being with God is eternal torment.

- Hinduism: Hinduism is similar to Buddhism. Salvation (or Moksha) is reached when the worshiper is freed from the cycle of reincarnation, and his spirit becomes one with god. One becomes free by ridding oneself of bad karma, the effect of evil action or evil intent. This can be done in three different ways: through selfless devotion to and service of a particular god, through understanding the nature of the universe, or by mastering the actions needed to fully appease the gods. In a religion with over a million different gods, there are differences of opinion regarding the nature of salvation. The advaita believe salvation occurs when one can strip away the false self and make the soul indistinguishable from that of god. The dualist insists that one's soul always retains its own identity even as it is joined with god.

- Islam: Islam is a take-off on the Christian/Judeo God. Muslims believe salvation comes to those who obey Allah sufficiently that good deeds outweigh the bad. Muslims hope that repeating what Muhammad did and said will be enough to get to heaven, but they also recite extra prayers, fast, go on pilgrimages, and perform good works in hope of tipping the scales. Martyrdom in service to Allah is the only work guaranteed to send a worshiper to paradise.

- Jainism: Jainism came to be in India about the same time as Hinduism and is very similar. One must hold the right belief, have the right knowledge, and act in the right manner. Only then can a soul be cleansed of karma. But in Jainism, there is no creator. There is no higher god to reach or lend aid. Salvation is man as master of his own destiny, liberated and perfect, filled with infinite perception, knowledge, bliss, and power.

- Jehovah's Witnesses: The teaching of the Watchtower Society is the epitome of the saying "a cult of Christianity is a religion that misinterprets the book of Revelation." Similar to Mormons, Jehovah's Witnesses teach different levels of heaven. The anointed are 144,000 who receive salvation by the blood of Christ and will rule with Him in paradise. They are the bride of Christ. To all others, Jesus' sacrifice only freed them from Adam's curse of original sin, and "faith" is merely the opportunity to earn their way to heaven. They must learn about Kingdom history, keep the laws of Jehovah, and be loyal to "God's government" (the 144,000 leaders, 9000 of whom are currently on the Earth). They must also spread the news about the Kingdom, including door-to-door proselytizing. Upon death, they will be resurrected during the millennial kingdom where they must continue a devout life. Only afterwards are they given the opportunity to formally accept Christ and live for eternity under the rule of the 144,000.

- Judaism: Jews believe that as individuals and as a nation, they begin reconciled to God. Through sin (individually or collectively) they can lose their salvation, but they can also earn it back through repentance, good deeds, and a life of devotion.

- Mormonism: Mormons believe their religion to be a derivative of Judeo/Christianity, but their reliance on extra-grace works belies this. They also have a different view of heaven. To reach the second heaven under "general salvation," one must accept Christ (either in this life or the next), and be baptized or be baptized by proxy through a living relative. To reach the highest heaven, one must believe in God and Jesus, repent of sins, be baptized in the church, be a member of the LDS church, receive the Holy Ghost by the laying on of hands, obey the Mormon "Word of Wisdom" and all God's commandments, and complete certain temple rituals including marriage. This "individual salvation" leads to the worshiper and his/her spouse becoming gods and giving birth to spirit children who return to Earth as the souls of the living.

- Roman Catholicism: Roman Catholics originally believed only those in the Roman Catholic Church could be saved. Joining the church was a long process of classes, rituals, and baptism. People who had already been baptized but were not members of the Roman Catholic Church had different requirements and may even already be considered Christians. Baptism is "normatively" required for salvation, but this can include "baptism of blood" (i.e.: martyrdom) or "baptism of desire" (wanting to be baptized really badly). From the catechism: "Those who die for the faith, those who are catechumens, and all those who, without knowing of the Church but acting under the inspiration of grace, seek God sincerely and strive to fulfill his will, are saved even if they have not been baptized." Despite the changes through the years, baptism (or the desire for baptism) is still required for salvation. Upon death, the souls of those who rejected Christ are sent to hell. The souls of those who accepted Christ and performed sufficient acts to be purified of sin go to heaven. Those who died in faith but did not complete the steps to be purified are sent to purgatory where they undergo temporary, painful punishment until their souls are cleansed. Purification by torment may be lessened by suffering during life and the offerings and prayers of others on the sinner's behalf. Once purification is complete, the soul may go to heaven.

- Scientology: Scientology is similar to Eastern religions in that salvation is achieved through knowledge of self and the universe. The "Thetan" (Scientology's answer to the soul) travels through several different lifetimes, attempting to expel painful and traumatic images that cause a person to act fearfully and irrationally. Once a Scientologist is "cleared" of these harmful images and becomes an "operating thetan," he/she is able to control thought, life, matter, energy, space, and time.

- Sikhism: Sikhism was created in reaction to the conflict between Hinduism and Islam, and carries on many of Hinduism's influences, although Sikhs are monotheistic. "Evil" is merely human selfishness. Salvation is attained by living an honest life and meditating on god. If performed sufficiently, the worshipper is released from the cycle of reincarnation and becomes one with god.

- Shinto: The afterlife in Shinto was originally a dire, Hades-like realm. Matters of the afterlife have now been transferred to Buddhism. This salvation is dependent on penance and avoiding impurity or pollution of the soul. Then one's soul can join those of its ancestors.

- Taoism: Like several other Eastern religions (Shinto, Chinese folk religions, Sikhism), Taoism adopted many of its afterlife principles from Buddhism. Initially, Taoists didn't concern themselves with worries of the afterlife and, instead, concentrated on creating a utopian society. Salvation was reached by aligning with the cosmos and receiving aid from supernatural immortals who resided on mountains, islands, and other places on Earth. The result was immortality. Eventually, Taoists abandoned the quest for immortality and took on the afterlife teachings of Buddhism.

- Unitarian-Universalism: Unitarians are allowed to and encouraged to believe anything they like about the afterlife and how to get there. Although in general, they believe people should seek enlightenment in this life and not worry too much about the afterlife.

- Wicca: Wiccans believe many different things about the afterlife, but most seem to agree that there is no need for salvation. People either live in harmony with the Goddess by caring for her physical manifestation (the Earth) or they don't, and their bad karma is returned to them three-fold. Some believe souls are reincarnated until they learn all their life lessons and become one with the Goddess. Some are so committed to following one's individual path that they believe individuals determine what will happen when they die; if worshippers think they're going to be reincarnated or sent to hell or joined with the goddess, they will be. Others refuse to contemplate the afterlife at all. Either way, they don't believe in sin or anything they need saving from.

- Zoroastrianism: Zoroastrianism may be the first religion that stated that the afterlife was dependent one's actions in life. There is no reincarnation, just a simple judgment four days after death. After a sufficient amount of time in hell, however, even the condemned can go to heaven. To be judged righteous, one can use knowledge or devotion, but the most effective way is through action.

78. Question: "Is Angelica Zambrano's testimony of experiencing heaven and hell biblically sound?"

Angelica Zambrano, an Ecuadorian teenage girl, claims that she was dead for 23 hours, during which she met Jesus Christ, and was led through hell and heaven so that she would be able to come back and warn people about the realities of the next life.

Angelica says that Jesus took her through hell first, and then gave her a glimpse of paradise. In the vision, Jesus told her, as they prepared to visit hell, "'Daughter, I will be with you. I will not leave you in that place and I am going to show you that place because there are many who know that hell exists, but they have no fear. They believe it's a game, that hell is a joke, and many don't know about it. That is why I am going to show you that place, because there are more that perish than those that are entering My glory.' When He said that, I could see tears streaming down to His garments. I asked Him, 'Lord, why are you crying?' He replied, 'Daughter, because there are more that perish, and I will show you this, so that you will go and tell the truth and so that you will not return to that place.'"

It is absolutely true that hell is real, and not a game or a joke, and it is also true that many people are going there *(Matthew 7:13; 25:46)*. It is true that Jesus laments over lost people *(Matthew 23:37)*. We know that He takes no pleasure in the death of the wicked *(Ezekiel 33:11)*. We also know that, in the last days, *"your sons and your daughters shall prophesy, and your young men shall see visions" (Acts 2:17)*, so the idea of Jesus weeping over those in hell is believable, and the possibility of a young person having an experience like Angelica's is not outside the bounds of Scripture.

That said, some of the elements of Angelica's account are unbiblical, or at least not sufficiently clear. For example, Angelica says that in the vision "I asked Him, 'Lord, why is my great-grandmother here? I don't know if she ever knew you. Why is she here in hell, Lord?' He replied, 'Daughter, she is here because she failed to forgive...Daughter, he who does not forgive, neither will I forgive him.' There are many other sins that, in Angelica's account, Jesus named as responsible for sending people to hell. It is true that sin is a symptom of an unsaved heart. But the account does not adequately explain the remedy: the grace of God through Jesus Christ is what saves us from the power and penalty of sin; justification and sanctification are accomplished for us, once for all, on the cross *(Hebrews 10:10, 14)*.

In the vision, Jesus also told Angelica that He is "coming for a holy people" and that "only the holy ones will see Me!" This is true, only those who have been made righteous by Christ *(2 Corinthians 5:21)* will be with Him in heaven *(Hebrews 12:23)*. But Angelica's account makes it sound as if holiness is a result of human effort. As Christians, we will pursue purity, obedience, and holiness, but we will do all those things as a result of what God has done for us, as a result of His grace, and the changed heart He has put within us *(Ephesians 2:8-9; 2 Corinthians 5:17)*. Angelica's testimony does not say anything that is explicitly against Scripture, but it neglects the idea of dependence on God for holiness, and it does not put enough emphasis on the assurance of salvation we have in Christ.

If we believe in the frightening vision of hell that is presented by this purported vision (and supported by Scripture), we will want to obey the Lord and live a holy life. But we will easily despair when we realize that we are unable to live a holy life. Thankfully, He has made it clear that we are to always depend on Him *(John 15:4)* to be able to bear the necessary fruit of salvation. He has also made it evident that He will forgive us when we sin *(1 John 1:9)*. Angelica's testimony leaves the reader with the feeling that if you commit a sin just before being hit by a bus, you will wind up in hell. This is not biblical. *"Surely there is not a righteous man on earth who does good and never sins" (Ecclesiastes 7:20)*.

It is important to note that Angelica Zambrano's testimony is only a human experience, and though much of her testimony does not contradict the Bible, the vision is not Scripture itself. It may be entirely a fabrication. There is really no way to know. Ultimately, with all purported visions and revelations, we must always "test everything" *(1 Thessalonians 5:21)*, only holding onto the good. It is only the Word of God that is inerrantly and authoritatively inspired. The fact that Angelica Zambrano's vision contains statements that are borderline unbiblical should give us serious caution against accepting any of it as being from God. What we can draw from it, however, is this crucial reality: a life of unrepentant sin, or a religious life of false holiness produced in our own efforts, without Jesus Christ to save us, will result in an eternity in hell, and hell is a very terrible place.

79. Question: "What is eternal death?"

In short, eternal death is the fate that awaits all people who ultimately reject God, reject the gospel of His Son, Jesus Christ, and remain in their sin and disobedience. Physical death is a one-time experience. Eternal death, on the other hand, is everlasting. It is a death that continues through eternity, a spiritual death that is experienced on a continual basis. Just as spiritual life, by grace through faith in Christ *(Ephesians 2:8-9)* is everlasting life, eternal death is never-ending.

The most important question to be answered is "Does the Bible teach the doctrine of eternal death?" If the Bible doesn't teach eternal death, then we can pack up and go home because there is no further debate on the issue. God's Word, the Bible, is the infallible rule of faith and practice, and as such we must believe and teach only what it clearly teaches, and the Bible clearly teaches the doctrine of eternal death. We can point to several passages that explicitly state this, but for our purposes, only three will be needed, one from the Old Testament and two from the New.

- *And many of those who sleep in the dust of the earth shall awake, some to everlasting life, and some to shame and everlasting contempt. (Daniel 12:2 ESV)*
- *And [the wicked] will go away into eternal punishment, but the righteous into eternal life. (Matthew 25:46 ESV)*
- *And if anyone's name was not found written in the book of life, he was thrown into the lake of fire. (Revelation 20:15 ESV)*. In verse 10, we are told that the Lake of Fire burns *"forever and ever."*

All three of these passages (and more could have been added) have as their main context the scene of final judgment. In other words, when Christ returns, three things will occur:

1. The general resurrection of "the living and the dead;"
2. the final judgment; and
3. the inauguration of the eternal state.

Each of these passages demonstrates that during the final judgment of all people, Jesus will separate the righteous from the wicked. The righteous will be ushered into the final state of glory, while the wicked will be sent to the lake of fire for eternal punishment and torment. Note too (particularly in the Daniel and Matthew passages) that the same adjective ("everlasting" or "eternal") is used to modify both "life" and "punishment/contempt." What is true about one (life) must be true about the other (punishment). Both are eternal and last forever.

The doctrine of eternal death is not a popular doctrine to teach or proclaim. To do so often opens one up to scorn and ridicule. However, we must not let that detract us from what the Bible so clearly teaches; namely, that due to our being born in sin and trespasses, we are under the just condemnation of God for our sin. If we do not embrace the saving message of Jesus Christ, we will perish in our sin and trespasses and be under God's just judgment for our sin, eternal death. This is a sobering doctrine and requires the utmost care and compassion in its presentation.

CPSIA information can be obtained at www.ICGtesting.com
Printed in the USA
BVOW02s0024220516

449059BV00017B/225/P